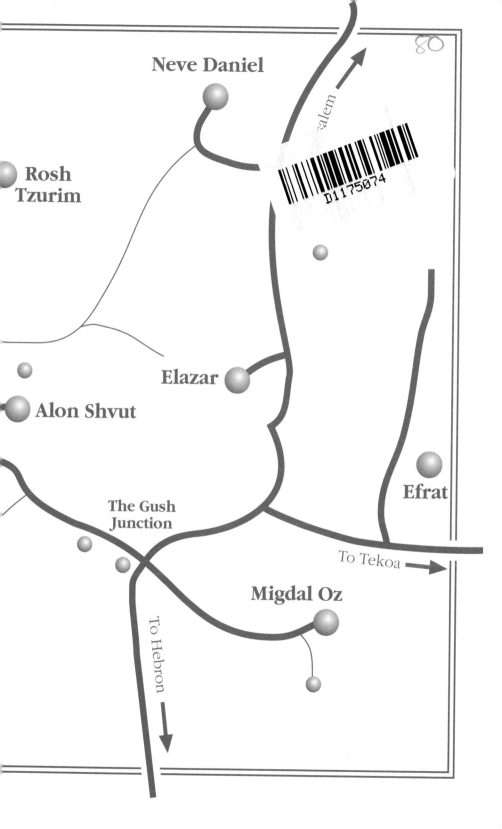

The Gush

The Gush

Center of Modern Religious Zionism

David Morrison

gefen
publishing house
JERUSALEM ◆ NEW YORK

Typesetting: Raphaël Freeman, Jerusalem Typesetting
Cover Design: Studio Paz

ISBN 965-229-309-1

1   3   5   7   9   8   6   4   2

Gefen Publishing House   Gefen Books
POB 36004, Jerusalem 91360, Israel   12 New Street, Hewlett, NY 11557, USA
972-2-538-0247   516-295-2805
orders@gefenpublishing.com   orders@gefenpublishing.com

www.israelbooks.com

Printed in Israel   *Send for our free catalogue*

Contents

Acknowledgments

I AM GRATEFUL to many people for the help and cooperation extended to me in the process of this work. First of all to Moshko, who agreed to the effort at the very beginning. Dr. Meyer Brayer brought Moshko and me together for that first meeting and, throughout the entire project, Dr. Brayer was my *madrich*. With an ever-ready smile and wonderful sprit, he greeted me on each visit to Yeshivat Har Etzion, set up many appointments and introduced me to all of the rich resources of the library and archives of the yeshiva.

Rabbis Amital, Lichtenstein and Riskin were generous with their time and encouragement. I was privileged to see up close the dedication to the highest levels of Torah study and living that they instill in their faculty and students.

I am deeply indebted to Esther Herskovics for her expert editing of the draft manuscripts of this book. Her sharp eye and deep knowledge of the subject material greatly enhanced the final product. Any remaining mistakes are entirely mine.

To the many wonderful people I interviewed, I am grateful for the opportunity they afforded me to hear about the exciting stories and experiences that make up an integral part of the Zionist dream.

Introduction

T HIS BOOK has meaning at a number of levels, each important in its own right, yet the whole constitutes more than the sum of its parts. To a great extent, the book is the story of the inspiration and determination of one man, Moshe Moscovic, affectionately know as "Moshko," to build a center of Jewish learning in Gush Etzion, on the land where so many of his comrades fell only one day before the declaration of the establishment of the State of Israel.

Yet, when I first consulted Moshko about the possibility of writing this book, he stressed with characteristic modesty that the story of Gush Etzion is the story of many dedicated men and women. More importantly, he emphasized that the story of Gush Etzion is not a war story, a memorial story; it is a story of a vibrant center of Jewish learning intended to reach out to all of Israel and, indeed, all of the world.

In the here and now, this book is a description of a religious *kehilla* – community – not well-known to Jews outside of Israel, and also little known to many secular Jews within the country. Jews and non-Jews who live with "truths" such as "all religious Jews do not serve in the army, are not dedicated to the State of Israel, and are not productive people" will find here a challenge to such "truths." The hope is that many readers, not familiar with this community, will come away with the same respect for it as do secular Jews in Israel who serve in the army with these religious men and women.

In terms of implications for the future, this book points to a group of Jews who are becoming, to an ever-growing extent, a central part of the leadership of the State of Israel. Their commitment to active engagement with all Israelis, along with a birth rate significantly higher than that of the secular population, makes their centrality to the future of Israel self-evident. Already, these religious Jews are represented in numbers equal to their percentage in the population in the elite Israeli air force; in the fighting units of *tzahal* – the Israeli army – they constitute a higher percentage than their representation in the Israeli population.

Looking back over thousands of years, it is clear that this religious community represents the continuity of Jewish life. The center of the world for the religious community in Gush Etzion, as well as religious communities everywhere, is the *beit-midrash* – a study hall for learning Gemarah – the oral tradition given by *Hashem* to Moses on Mount Sinai. This was the center of the world for our patriarchs who studied in the *beit-midrash* of Shem and Ever, the center of the world in Jerusalem before the fall of the first and second Temples, and it was the center of the world at Sura and Pumbedita where the rabbis established yeshivas after the Romans expelled the Jews from Jerusalem.

The community that is the focus of this book is part of the *kippa s'ruga* community. The Hebrew words *kippa s'ruga* mean "crocheted skullcap." This designation is not only a description of the type of *kippa* worn by the men of this community, but also a term frequently employed to differentiate this community from the "black" community, those religious Jews who wear black coats and hats and are commonly referred to as *charedim*.

While the differentiation between the "black" or "*charedi*" community and the *kippa s'ruga* community is more apparent than real, it is a heuristic division. The label "ultra-religious," often applied to the *charedi* world, is not accurate; the adherence to the Torah and its mitzvot is an absolute and equal value in both communities; the *charedim* do not pray more than the *kippa s'ruga* community. The most accurate differentiating adjective is "insular." The *charedi* community seeks to minimize the exposure of its members to any culture other than its own. Thus, the community prefers its members to study rather than be exposed to the vicissitudes of the work force and the army. The *kippa s'ruga* community of Gush Etzion and the rest of Israel, while steadfast in its adherence to Torah, not only does not fear secular Israeli culture, but believes in actively engaging it and, indeed, the world in general.

This book is not a history of the communities that Moshko created, but a snapshot. There is no pretense to objectivity from afar; I liked what I knew in advance of encountering this community, so invited myself in for a closer look. Now, full of admiration and respect for people who gave me a warm welcome, I present this snapshot to the reader.

The reader will note that, throughout this book, titles of respect are used. When referring to the rabbis, the Hebrew title *rav* is used; thus "Rav Amital," instead of "Amital," which is common in writing about historical figues. This style is employed because it was unthinkable for me not to do so. How then, for the "central character," can I simply write "Moshko?" The answer is that, for everyone who knows Moshe Moscovic, it is clear that "Moshko" is not just a name, but a word said with ultimate respect and love. It is my greatest hope that I portray this giant of a leader in a way realistic enough to impress on the reader the name, the title, the respect, and the love that are all rolled up in the word "Moshko."

Moshe Moskovic – "Moshko"

Chapter I
Moshko

"**H**ERE WILL BE a yeshiva, Shulamit!" Her father almost exploded in excitement, his eyes scouring every inch of the Hebron Hills. Shulamit's emotions were torn between the pulsating enthusiasm of her beloved father and concerns about the man she would soon marry. Yaacov had been injured in the just concluded Six Day War, and she had not yet seen him.

Moshko, as her father is affectionately called, knew well the forbidding, craggy terrain he surveyed. Seeped into every fiber of his fertile mind were visions of *Avraham avinu* – our father Abraham – who had welcomed guests in this very area. Herds of sheep had wandered on this soil tended by David, their loving shepherd. It was here that the Maccabees had stood their ground against the Greeks.

From Jerusalem south to Bethlehem, the mountains proudly rising toward the heavens are known as the Jerusalem Hills. Continuing further south, at yet more lofty altitudes, they become the Hebron Hills.

This was the land bequeathed by Jacob to his son Judah. Judah, whose three older brothers were rebuked by Jacob for their violence, was praised: "Judah – you, your brothers shall acknowledge; your hand will be at your enemies' nape; your father's sons will prostrate themselves to you. A lion cub is Judah; from the prey, my son, you elevated yourself." Foreseeing the future when, from David forward, the House of Judah would lead Israel, and ultimately bring forth the *mashiach*, the Redeemer, Jacob continued: "The scepter shall not depart from Judah" (*Bereishit*, 49:8–10).

David secluded himself in these hills when he fled from Saul. And to these hills, "the men of Judah came, and there they anointed David king over the house of Judah" (*Samuel II*, 2:4).

To make his dream of a center for Jewish education a reality would require hard work, but Moshko was no stranger to what many considered "impossible" endeavors. Born Moshe Moskovic in Bratislava, Czechoslovakia, in 1929, he was the second of four children. Bratislava is also known as Pressburg, the city of the Chatam Sofer, a great leader of Orthodox Jewry in the early 1800s. Well established and financially well-to-do, Moshko's father nonetheless saw the danger in Hitler's rise to power and prepared his family to move to Palestine.

"I emphasize that my father was a Zionist," Moshko explains, "but it is difficult today to explain it – why he decided to come to Palestine. The neighbors came and said: 'Maybe you should send him to a doctor. Something is not right. He is a wealthy man with a big factory for bicycles and sewing machines and decides to liquidate everything and go to Palestine, leaving his family here.' I also cannot explain this because, while he was a member of the Mizrachi Zionists, he was not a man of big ideas, nor was he a big rabbi. He just decided that in Europe there was no chance for Jews."

Moshko's father did not succeed in convincing his family. He went ahead and sent for them one and a half years later, in 1935. The daughter of one of his brothers accompanied Moshko's family; the rest remained in Europe and most were killed by the Germans. Two cousins survived the war and came to Israel. Thus, of seventy family members only three survived.

At age fifteen, Moshko decided he wanted to work in agriculture, which made his father very happy. He applied to the agricultural school in Mikve Yisrael, but did not have money for tuition. His mother took him to Henrietta Szold, the legendary head of Hadassah and Youth Aliyah. When told the school only accepted new immigrants, Moshko's mother persisted, asking: "Is it my son's fault that we came here five years ago?" Henrietta Szold relented, and Moshko received a stipend for the Mikve Yisrael school.

Eventually, Moshko's father bought land in Beit She'an. "Why in Beit She'an?" Moshko reflects, "Because in the Gemarah it is written: "If paradise is in the land of Israel, its gate is in Beit She'an" (*Eruvin*, 19a). This sounds so strange and romantic. He could have bought apartments in Tel Aviv. But, no, he bought land in Beit She'an."

In 1929, during the Arab riots, many Jews in Hebron were murdered and many others withdrew from the area. However, a private entrepreneur, Shmuel Holtzman, bought a great deal of land in the Hebron hills and founded a new settlement. In a play on words, the settlement, Kfar Etzion, bears his name, since both "*holtz*" (in Yiddish) and "*etz*" (in Hebrew) mean wood.[1] However, the Arabs struck again in 1936 in a series of murderous riots that went on for three years, and in 1937 the new village had to be evacuated.

The land was bought by the Jewish National Fund in 1942, and government settlement officials turned to *Kvutzat Avraham*, a religious settlement group then in Samaria, to make their new home in Kfar Etzion. These young people were originally organized as a youth movement of *HaPoel HaMizrahi* – a religious pioneering labor movement – in Lvov, Poland, in 1934.

Many students came to Palestine in the wake of World War II, when Moshko was part of a large group studying at Mikve Yisrael. Dating back to 1870, Mikve Yisrael – was established by Frenchman Charles Netter on behalf of the Alliance Israélite Universelle. Against the wishes of the kibbutz organization that insisted they must join one of the established kibbutzim, a nucleus of students

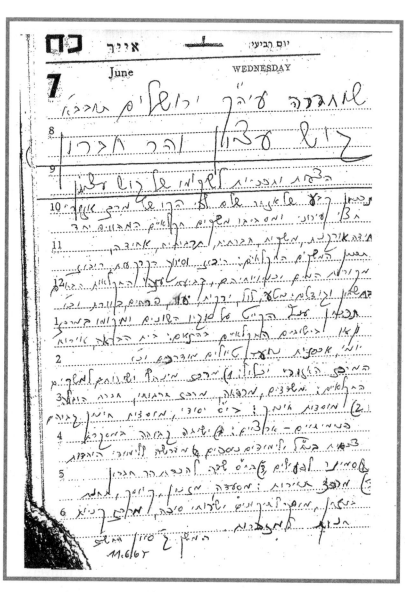

Moshko's Diary of June 7, 1567

The Gush – Moshko

WEDNESDAY, 28 IYAR, 7 JUNE 1967

JERUSALEM THE HOLY CITY WAS RELEASED
GUSH EZION AND THE HEBRON HILL

SUGGESTIONS AND PLANS FOR THE REBUILDING OF GUSH ETZION

- Planning of a whole area by the lines of a regional letter, semi urban surrounded by agricultural units who together form an organic unit, economically, socially and culturally.
- Planning the agricultural units, concentrating the land, water supplies
- Planning a variety of tourist and recreation facilities and placing it in the center and/or within the agricultural communities: a guest house, B&B, a youth hostel, a center for hikes for youth, etc.
- The regional center will include:

  1) a business center to service the agricultural settlements, offices, infirmary, cultural center, trucking services.

  2) Educational institutions: Elementary school, high education facilities – with dorms for students from all over the country.

  A. A High Yeshiva in a military framework (NACHAL) and other studies.

  B. A Jewish study academy.

  C. A seminar for activists.

  D. A school for teaching Har Hebron.

  3) A tourist center: A restaurant, a snack bar, kiosk, a gas station, a car garage, a shopping center and a Souvenir store.

Continued: 3 Sivan 11 June, 1967

decided to go out on their own to set up an independent kibbutz. In 1945, when the students went out for training, they were told that if they insisted on being independent, there was only one place for them, and that place was in the craggy hills adjacent to Kfar Etzion.

Like the members of *Kvutzat Avraham* who had established Kfar Etzion, Moshko and the others who set up Massuot one mile to the northwest were also affiliated with *HaPoel HaMizrachi*. While *Kvutzat Avraham* stemmed from Poland, Moshko's group originated in Hungary and Czechoslovakia.

Thus the students of a prestigious agricultural school decided to move to a rocky area with forbidding, steep slopes, not the most hospitable terrain for agriculture. Massuot was soon to become Massuot Yitzhak, in honor of Israel's second chief rabbi, Yitzhak Herzog.

Rabbi Herzog, selected as Israel's chief rabbi after the death of Rabbi Avraham Yitzhak Kook, was visiting America when WWII broke out. He was determined to return to his people despite the advice of many who tried to dissuade him. The waterways from America to Europe were endangered by German U-boats, and Field-Marshal Rommel was at the gates of Egypt. Because Rabbi Herzog braved the dangers of a return to *Eretz Yisrael*, the *Keren Kayemet* (Jewish National Fund) – the land purchase and development agency founded in 1902 – wanted to name the new settlement in his honor. The members were proud to change Massuot to Massuot Yitzhak.

Approximately six months later, Ein Tzurim, a third religious settlement, was established, followed after another half a year by Revadim, a kibbutz of the secular, anti-religious movement *HaShomer HaTzair*. Thus was completed the bloc of four settlements in the area known as Gush Etzion.

Life in "the Gush" was extremely difficult. Clearing rocks from the land was demanding physical labor, and there was no natural water source; water had to be brought from Jerusalem. In 1948, as in 1929 and 1937, the Arabs attacked, determined to drive the Jews out of the area. The four settlements of Gush Etzion were isolated, with no clear lines of supply. In retrospect, Moshko can see that there was no chance to stand up to the Arab onslaught. First the children were evacuated to Jerusalem, then the women. Moshko tried to keep up with developments from Cyprus where he had been sent as a leader and trainer of refugees who had escaped the Nazis, yet were held behind barbed wire by the British.

In 1948 Rabbi Yitzhak Herzog came to the rescue of the settlement that bears his name and the three neighboring settlements. When it became clear that Gush Etzion could not hold out against the Arab onslaught, Rabbi Herzog contacted the International Red Cross. Until then, whenever Jewish positions were overrun, the Arabs simply killed everyone. Rabbi Herzog reached King Abdullah through the Red Cross, and he agreed that the Arab Legion for the first time would take prisoners.

Moshko remembers that, when it was decided to evacuate the women, the Arabs would not agree to safe passage. They would only agree to let the cows out. In a truck, between cows, his wife was able to get to Jerusalem.

Now, in June 1967, Moshko was flooded with all these memories as he surveyed the area with his daughter who had been evacuated from this spot at age one. He embraced her and set his eyes to the future. "Your Yaakov will recover from his wounds, and the two of you will marry and come here to raise your family. This time, with God's help, you will never have to leave."

"The Alon – Oak tree" in Gush Etzion from 1948–1967 the only visible symbol of home for Jews who were expelled in 1948 and who could return only after the 1967 war

Chapter II
Rebuilding

L EADING FROM the main road of Massuot Yitzhak was a small path to an Arab village. The *muhktar* of the Arab village was a man who enjoyed walking the path to the Jewish settlement to show he was the true master of the area. "You won't stay here very long," he told them confidently. "Just like we expelled you in 1929, so will we do it again." And in 1948 they did.

After the fall of the Gush, the Arabs destroyed all of the Jewish houses and even uprooted the trees. One tree, an *alon* – oak tree – stood tall as a symbol of the Jewish settlements that had fallen. "We also had some types of European olive trees that the Arabs did not have," Moshko relates. "When we returned in 1967, we found some of these trees in Arab villages." The oak tree remained in its original place.

The scars of the 1948 war were deep and wide. Gush Etzion suffered two hundred and fifty people killed in action. Until this day, despite all of Israel's wars, there is no single battle site where so many Jews died. When the survivors discussed their future, it was clear that the back-breaking work and the large number killed in action had taken a heavy physical and psychological toll. Many

9

former members of the four Gush settlements did not want to continue kibbutz life, and they scattered to many different places.

The War of Liberation was very harsh, and many people know
about the fall of Gush Etzion. But the story of this settlement bloc,
Moshko insists, should not be remembered just for its tragedy. "I
want to emphasize that the war was terrible and cruel, but that is not
the real story of Gush Etzion. We didn't choose the war. We chose
to come to that place to establish ourselves despite the adverse
conditions. Much of our revered history took place there. But the
real story is one of Zionism and of an important center of Jewish
education."

After the Six Day War in 1967, Moshko and some friends returned to the area to decide what should be done. "Suddenly we saw
a caravan of Arabs on donkeys and an old man stopped beside us.
He looked at me and asked: 'Do you know me?' I said no. He said 'I
am the *muhktar* of Jabba. You remember what I said to you – that
we would expel you. This time I realize you have returned to stay.
You are planning houses of stone. Whoever builds houses of stone,
that is a sign they will stay."

However, more than half of the surviving members of Massuot
Yitzhak and Ein Tzurim decided not to return. They were now well-
established in their new communities. Moshko remains a member
of the relocated Massuot Yitzhak, situated between Ashdod and
Ashkelon, to this day. He recalls the days of longing between 1948
and 1967. "For the nineteen years between 1948 and 1967, we held
ceremonies and would look from afar at the single oak tree left
standing at Gush Etzion. We would dream of the day when we
would go back and raise our children there, returning them to their
heritage. The truth is that, while we dreamed of this, we did not
really expect it to happen – not in our lifetime."

Two days after the Six Day War, Moshko and other members
of Massuot Yitzhak were invited by the army to come to the area.
"It is difficult to describe it. On the one hand, we were joyous that

we had won the war, and that Jerusalem and the Gush were back in our hands. On the other hand, everything that we once had there was completely destroyed." Moshko's dream burned inside him, and his words leaped from his soul as he addressed his friends:

> Those of us who remained alive did so only because of a miracle from heaven. We have an obligation and that is to build the Gush anew. Today there is no chance to start new kibbutzim here. The ground is not fertile, and kibbutzim are already going out of fashion. We already have Massuot Yitzhak in the south. Let us go a bit more to the center of the Gush and establish a large *yishuv* of a hundred and fifty families who will do whatever kind of work they want. Some will work here, some in Jerusalem. We will establish educational institutions. We will have no direct connection to the other three kibbutzim, but will be a community unto ourselves. I want to establish a *hesder* yeshiva here.

On army service for Yeshiva students, Moshko is unequivocal:

> Part of the *charedi* world does not go to the army because of the fear that their students will be confused by what they see in the secular world. Our students in *hesder* yeshivas are not ordinary students. They are the elite in terms of intelligence, commitment to Torah and strength of character. It isn't just that the army does not harm our students, it helps them. They are exposed to a larger world, and that exposure strengthens them, matures them. They see they can be an example for other young men. We should prefer to live in a world where we don't need the army; but given the reality, it is essential that we be part of that larger world.

Moshko is fully cognizant of the reality of Israeli demographics – that most of the population is secular:

We have to do everything we can not only to be a part of *Klal Yis-rael*, but to contribute to it. We know the reality that the majority of the population is not religious. It is important that we be the bridge, the connection between all the people of Israel. Only we can do that, because we live in the real world, the modern world. We are part of the scientific world, the economy, and we can show the secular world that Torah is not something with horns, that we live in normal communities with important organizations, that we show the best of the religious world. And we do so not by making speeches, but by personal example.

The Hebrew word *"hesder"* means "arrangement." A *hesder* yeshiva is a yeshiva that, by special arrangement with the Israeli government, has a five-year program of religious study and army service. The idea arose after the Six Day War. During the five years, students serve eighteen months in the army in two separate stints interspersed with intensive yeshiva learning.

Moshko, with the help of Rabbi Yitzhak Herzog, managed to get an important grant from the Rothschild Foundation. Both government and private money were raised and Yeshivat Har Etzion was built.

The plan that Moshko presented to the government was one for a settlement that would be an educational center. He suggested that the new community be founded on the basis of *b'nei beitcha* – where everyone owns his own house and land. That was a revolutionary idea in Israel. The government balked at the idea of establishing a yeshiva, but Moshko convinced them of its importance as the spiritual basis for the community.

"I told them from the beginning that the basis of the new settlement would be a yeshiva – a yeshiva that constitutes the reason for a settlement. I had good relations with Yigal Alon. We met when he was head of Palmach – the elite underground guerilla unit established in 1948." Now, after the Six Day War, Alon was Minister of Education and they met again. Alon was receptive to Moshko's idea. There was no political argument about the Gush. "I simply told them I want to return home."

Moshko prepared a handwritten document describing his plans. He wrote that he wanted to establish a yeshiva in the Gush. Alon added the words: "and a *yishuv.*" "Alon was secular Jew, a socialist, but he was not anti-religious. He saw in the Gush the realization of Zionism as he viewed it – settlement, defense and education. He said it would help protect Jerusalem."

Moshko's deeply-held belief is that Zionism is built on three things: *aliyah* (immigration), settlement and education. Some of the people who came to live in Alon Shevut, the new community which replaced Massuot Yitzhak, were *olim chadashim* – new immigrants. They were pioneers who established a new settlement. They brought other people who came on *aliyah* to live and raise their children there. The third leg of Zionism – education – is crucial. As Moshko explains: "I strongly believe that the people of Israel have a role in the world, and that we, as a religious community, have a task of our own. If we want to remain a Jewish community we must invest in education, above all in education for the leadership of the Jewish people."

Harav Yehuda Amital

Chapter III
Rav Yehuda Amital

I N HIS SEARCH for someone to head the Torah education of Alon Shevut, Moshko was prescient in choosing Yehuda Amital, a rabbi who, already in his youth, had made a name for himself as an ardent religious Zionist. Rav Amital had served in the Haganah – the pre-state "official" underground fighting unit, and in the Israeli Defense Force (IDF). He was born in 1924 in Grosswardein, in an area called Transylvania, then part of Hungary. After Budapest, Transylvania had the largest Hungarian community, with approximately 30,000 Jews, both Orthodox and Reform.

Yehuda Amital was the first of three children, with a sister two years younger, and a brother twelve years younger. His parents, both Hungarian, were "modern people," Rav Amital relates. "My father was an accountant who did not wear a beard. I went to a secular school for four grades, then to cheder and afterwards yeshiva. A Talmud scholar, Chaim Yehuda Levi, came to our city from Lithuania. He was later killed by the Nazis. He introduced a system of study that was new for Hungary, a system more analytical, more in depth."

When Rav Amital reached Israel, in 1944, he was shown a letter he had written to his grandfather, in Hebrew, at age 13. Most of his father's family had left for Israel before World War II. Hungarian was spoken in the Amital home when he was growing up, but "when I saw the letter I wrote at age 13 in Hebrew, I realized I had been given a good education."

Rav Amital remembers well the discussions that took place in anticipation of the Nazi invasion of Hungary:

> We sat, young men and young women, and talked about what we should do. There were those who said we should run away, leave Hungary. I was very pessimistic. The Nazis were conquering one place after another. I said there was nothing to do; we should be ready to die *al kiddush Hashem* – for the sanctity of God's name. My friends were very angry at me. This is important because of what came afterwards. When I came to Israel and entered the Hebron Yeshiva in Jerusalem, one day a friend and I went on a field trip to Kfar Etzion. In the field, I saw a man who said: 'Yehuda, is that you?' It was a friend of mine from Hungary, a relative of Rabbi Lau. He began to shout at me: 'You survived, you were saved! You told us to be prepared to die, and you were saved.' I responded: 'Yes, of what am I guilty?' The next question he asked me was: 'Yehuda, did you remain religious?' I answered yes. This is the argument I had later with Abba Kovner. Who has the most difficult task – me who has to wrestle with his faith in God after the Holocaust, or you who has to wrestle with his faith in man after the Holocaust?

When the Nazis arrived, the Amital family had already been taken to a ghetto. Rav Amital was sent to a work camp. He learned quickly that reporting sick was not a way out of work, but a prescription for transport to a death camp. "One day, a certain guard came and had everyone take off their clothes. The sick ones were sent to Auschwitz. Those with *protektzia* – connections – went on Kastner's train to Israel."

By chance, Rav Amital was assigned to a work force that went into his home city. They were ordered to remove all property from Jewish homes. Rav Amital remembers:

> I arrived and discovered letters of my Rabbi, and we also found a small Sefer Torah that we were able to take with us. We were 200–250 men who kept kosher. We ate only dry bread. Thirty of us were taken to work on some farm. We had a yellow badge. Those Jews who had converted wore a white badge. Rumor had it that those who converted would be returned to their families. Many Jews were tempted by this and converted. There was an assistant commander, an officer in the Hungarian army, who allowed us to have vegetables and to rest on Shabbat.

One day, with the High Holy Days approaching, the work force received orders to return to the city. It was pouring rain, and they trudged with difficulty through the deep, thick mud. They heard shouts that the Russians were nearing.

> We took the Sefer Torah with us and took turns guarding it. We felt the Torah was watching over us. Then we saw thousands of people running in the direction of the Russians. When the guard of our group went to phone his base, we ran away. After a few hours, some of us were caught and returned to the officer. He said, 'Now you will have to be tried.' Then we came to a bridge and heard shooting only a few meters away. The officer ran away and we stayed. Ten or twelve of us went into a community house. This was on Erev Yom Kippur. We waited for the Russians. In a basement, we found a little bread to eat. We ate, then we prayed. From there we went to what had been the home of a friend of mine. We heard noise outside and realized it was a German patrol. They shouted and said that if we did not come out, they would blow the place up. Some went out, and I heard someone shout:

'Yehuda, come on out, nothing will happen to you.' My friend and
I stayed in the house. The Germans came in and checked every
room except the one we were in. It was one of those miracles.

Shortly thereafter, a Hungarian commander came and told
the Germans he needed his Jewish workers and they should leave
them alone. He rounded up close to one hundred Jewish men into
a work force, and they worked day after day, very near the front.
Again the Russians drew near. The Hungarian officer said to his
Jewish workers: "Until now, I watched over you. Now you must
watch over me."

Then Rav Amital heard "a huge *balagan*" – din of confusing
noises. The Russians came down the road with horses and wagons,
with many people trailing behind. For him and his friends, the
nightmare was over.

Rav Amital and a good friend decided to go to Israel via Rumania. There was a short period of time when the British declared
that whoever arrived in Istanbul would get a certificate to enter
Eretz Yisrael. A certain number of certificates were allotted to different sectors, such as labor groups and religious groups. In addition, there were also general certificates. Rav Amital was given an
unaffiliated certificate.

On a small, crowded boat, "we sat likes sardines." Rav Amital
and his friend sailed from Bucharest to Istanbul, and from Istanbul,
they took trains through Syria and Lebanon. On the second day of
Chanukah, Rav Amital reached the soil of Eretz Yisrael.

Reunited with his father's family who had sailed for Palestine
before the war, Rav Amital received the news that his immediate
family was dead – his parents, his sister and his brother. "I heard
that my sister survived the Nazis, but died of typhus just after the
war. I had no confirmation of this. I found out the date of the transport that took my parents to Auschwitz, and I set the date as their
yahrzeit to say Kaddish. Rav Amital sees meaning in his arrival in

Israel: "I have always felt that I arrived in Israel for a reason – not to represent myself, but all those who died in the *Shoah* – Holocaust – and could not get here. Once, around 1984, a group of some one hundred to one-hundred fifty people who survived the Holocaust came to the yeshiva. They toured the whole campus. I said to them that my impetus to establish the yeshiva was my sense of *shlichut* – my mission. I felt that I represented those who remained in Europe. That is what gives me strength."

A book by Moshe Maya, published in 2002, captures well the influence of the Holocaust on Rav Amital.[2] A particularly striking statement by Rav Amital, which Maya cites, is the following:

> Throughout the years, a terrible thought has pursued me: Millions of Jews were killed in the Holocaust. I was saved. Was I saved because the Holy One, Blessed be He, chose me to be brought out of the Holocaust, or was it perhaps a period of *hester panim* – "hiding of God's face?" …If I knew that Hashem had chosen me, this would place a very heavy responsibility upon me. On one hand, I am not certain I could bear it. But on the other hand, I would give everything in the world for the Holy One to have extended His mercy to me, personally…I am a simple and insignificant person, but when I was saved, I felt that I must have extra strength, to fill also the place of those who are no longer with us. This gave me the courage to do things that are beyond my personal abilities.

While there exists, in this statement, a clear sense of mission, Rav Amital rejects out-of-hand the concept of making this mission into a new theology as have important religious thinkers like Rabbi Yitz Greenberg and Doctor Emil Fackenheim. Rav Amital does not accept the idea that the Holocaust imposes any type of obligation.

Rav Amital was greatly influenced by the works of Rav Avraham Yitzhak HaCohen Kook, Israel's first Chief Rabbi. Rav Kook held that *aliyah* to Eretz Yisrael was part of God's divine plan of redemption, and he saw in secular, even anti-religious Jews, part of God's plan. He believed that yeshiva education should include secular subjects.

When Rav Amital was sent to the work camp, he took a Bible, a book of *mishnas*, and a small volume of Rav Kook's writings. "I saw in his writings, a new way, a deeper way of relating to Eretz Yisrael."

Twenty years old when he arrived in Jerusalem, Rav Amital studied in the Hebron Yeshiva, one of the oldest, and still one of the most important yeshivas in Jerusalem. The Hebron Yeshiva was patterned on the European style, and he was comfortable studying there. After six months, he went to find work in Pardes Hanna. "I didn't find a job, but I found a wife." She was the daughter of the Rabbi of Pardes Hanna, the brother-in-law of the revered Rav Aaron Kotler. Rav Kotler had fled the Nazis and had come to the United States where he headed up the *Vaad Hatzalah* – rescue committee – during World War II. He was also the president of the Supreme Council of Agudat Yisrael.

For Rav Amital, there was never any conflict between being religious and defending Israel. At the Hebron Yeshiva, the students were recruited by the Haganah, as well as by *Lechi* and *Etzel*, the underground movements headed by followers of Zeev Jabotinsky. Rav Amital made his choice: "I joined Haganah because it was the 'official' underground. I went in the middle of the night to the place they told me and said the code word I had been given. They told me to go upstairs. Someone else there also asked for the code, then told me to go up further. I went into a room. There was a bed sheet hung up. Someone was behind it. He asked why I had come. I told him I wanted to join the Haganah and contribute to the founding of the State."

At the time of the War of Independence, in 1948, Rav Amital was integrated into the new Israeli army, serving in the Galili Di-

vision. When the officers saw on his papers that he had been in
the Haganah, they wanted to make him the commander of a unit.
Most of the people in the unit had arrived in Israel straight from
British detention camps in Cyprus and had no military training
whatsoever. "They believed that if I had been in the Haganah, I
must know how to use a rifle. I felt I was not at that level, so I said
no," Rav Amital recounts with a smile: "I made a mistake, because
the one who became commander knew less than I."

When his unit arrived in Latrun, Rav Amital was put in charge
of the walkie-talkie because of his knowledge of Hebrew. Just before
Shavuot, there was a cease-fire. "It was Erev Shavuot, and I realized I had no wine for Kiddush. One of the religious soldiers had
some wine with him. I told him to tell everyone we would recite
Kiddush."

After the war, Rav Amital became an instructor in a yeshiva in
Rehovot, then went to Jerusalem to teach. His son was born two
years after his marriage. In the course of time, the couple had four
daughters, three of whom live in Alon Shevut today.

Jerusalem is the center of the Jewish universe. How did Rav
Yehuda Amital become the founding rosh yeshiva in the rocky,
sparsely populated area that is Gush Etzion?

> Came Moshko who said we want to start a yeshiva in Gush Etzion
> and want you to be the rosh yeshiva. I didn't know him. He felt
> a need to establish a yeshiva there. I said why are you coming to
> me? I was not famous. Many people told me it wasn't worth it. I
> realized they had no bank account. They had only the will to do
> something. Moshko's enthusiasm is infectious. So I came.

When he interviewed students who were looking for a place to
study, many wanted to know what was special about this particular
yeshiva. Rav Amital always told them a chassidic story that for him
has deep meaning – a story that is forever engraved in the soul

of the hundreds of students who have studied with the first rosh yeshiva of Yeshiva Har Etzion.

> Rav Shneur Zalman, the first Chabad Rabbi and author of *Tanya* – a major treatise on kabbala – had to leave his city because of persecution. He traveled to another city with his grandson, the Tzemach Tzedek, who would become the third Lubavitcher Rebbe, and his infant son. They took an apartment with three rooms. In those days, there were no hallways; each room led to the next. One day Rav Zalman sat in one room and studied. In the middle room sat the Tzemach Tzedek studying Gemarah. In the third room was the infant in his cradle. Suddenly the infant began to cry. His father, the Tzemach Tzedek, lost in his studies, did not hear the child and did not notice Shneur Zalman pass through his room on the way to comfort the infant. He held the boy until he was calmed then placed him back in his cradle, staying in the room until the child fell asleep. Then he went to the Tzemach Tzedek's room and said: If one studies and does not hear the cry of a Jewish child, that is a sign that his studies are flawed; something is amiss.

"That is the message of the yeshiva," Rav Amital asserts. "We will study Torah, but we will be alert to the cries of an infant, which is to say, to the needs of the Jewish people."

Yeshivat Har Etzion began to function in 1967. A few buildings left standing by the Arabs, as well as some tin buildings of the Arab Legion, constituted the "campus." In the summer it was steaming hot, and in the winter the cold was penetrating. The big supporter of the yeshiva in the government was Yigal Alon. "Moshko sat with Alon who drafted a proposal for the government. The document proclaimed that the government will establish a *hesder* yeshiva in Gush Etzion." Rav Amital had his doubts about government support. He went to some of the ministers who responded: "Don't worry, just trust me."

Rav Amital was not reassured that the government would officially support the Yeshiva. This was at the time of the national unity government formed just prior to the Six Day War, the first time that Menachem Begin, head of the Likud opposition party, served in the government. Rav Amital knew that Begin, while not a religious Jew, in a formal sense, was very traditional and personally connected to Judaism:

> I told my secretary to call Begin and tell him that the rosh yeshiva of Har Etzion wants to talk to him, today. She called and he said he had to attend a meeting of Herut, his political party, and wasn't able to do it. I told her to tell him I must see him right away, before the government next meets. Begin said: 'If Rav Amital is prepared to come to me at 10 o'clock tonight, I am willing to meet with him.' I went to Tel Aviv. He lived in a modest apartment, and was sitting at a small table. He was reassuring, and I trusted him. We got the confirmation from the government. This was the first time, and the last time, that the government established a yeshiva.

In October 1969, in an emotion-charged ceremony, the *even pina* – cornerstone – was placed in the craggy, unsettled area from which would arise the majectic profile of Yeshivat Har Etzion. The deputy prime minister, Yigal Alon, spoke of twenty years of hearts burning to return to the Gush. "Establishing a new yishuv in place of those which were stolen from us is the most constructive revenge possible…a military presence is not a constructive alternative to Jewish settlement."

Many of those who would be in the first class of the yeshiva attended the ceremony in their army uniforms, as they had participated enthusiastically in the Six Day War. They heard their rosh yeshiva, Rav Amital, speak of the necessity to mesh the power of the spirit with the power of the body to establish a yishuv steeped in Jewish values that would also serve as an important link in the security belt around Jerusalem. In a reference to the *akedah*, the binding of Isaac, Moshko spoke poignantly of building a new home, greater than the first, a home that would arise through the *akedah* not of a single person, but of many.

When students first came to Yeshivat Har Etzion, Rav Amital liked to ask them: "What do you see, what do you see?" They looked at the deserted area and shrugged their shoulders. Rav Amital would tell them what he saw: "I see the mountain full of houses. In the middle is a *beit midrash*. Children are running around and playing. One of the rabbis who had been a student of mine, took me aside and said: Rav Amital, you bluffer, how can you tell such stories to these children." When the vision was realized, that rabbi never dared to come visit the yeshiva.

When the yeshiva was on the drawing board, Rav Amital received a phone call telling him that a wealthy Jew from Toronto wanted to see him. He was told the man might even give a million dollars to the yeshiva. There was a Wolfson Foundation plan for building in Jerusalem, and the United States government was willing to give some money. Knowing the United States position that Gush Etzion was "occupied territory," Rav Amital doubted the American government's willingness to contribute anything in the Gush. "I was used to pleading for money; but it wasn't my experience that someone sought me out to give me a million dollars." He met the potential donor at the King David Hotel in Jerusalem, and told him of his doubts. The man said, somewhat cavalierly, "So build a yeshiva in Jerusalem.' I said thank you very much, but we are establishing a yeshiva in Gush Etzion. In the end, he gave a million dollars of his own to the yeshiva."

The Israeli government built houses in Alon Shevut. The first *beit midrash* was established in a big warehouse. The majestic edifice that stands today was dedicated after the Yom Kippur War. At that time, in 1973, there were 150 students at Yeshivat Har Etzion. Sadly, eight of the yeshiva students were killed in the war.

Rav Amital recalls how a visit to Alon Shevut by Moshe Dayan provided him with *proteksia* (influence) on one of his field visits during the Yom Kippur War:

> On Succoth Moshe Dayan came to visit, along with the *ramatcal*, Military Chief of Staff, Dado, and their entourage. Dayan said: 'We want you to enlarge your settlement.' He pointed to our *eruv* and asked: 'What is that wire?' I told him that within the wire one could carry things on Shabbat, but not outside it. He told us we could build up to "that wire." He went to the succah and, after a while someone came and said that Minister Dayan wants to see me. I joined him in the succah, and he told me to sit beside him. I sat between him and Dado. He asked: 'What is the law of succah – is it like a synagogue or a house?' I told him it was like a house. He smiled and took off his kippa. Someone took a picture and it appeared in Haaretz. I cut out the picture and put it in my wallet.
>
> During the Yom Kippur War I went to the Sinai to visit the troops. I went once with Rav Lichtenstein and Dr. Brayer. Some of our soldiers, including my son, had already crossed the canal, and I wanted to go to the other side. A soldier there said it wasn't possible. I asked if we could get permission from his commander. He said, the commander is very firm about this; there is no chance. I went to the commander and said: 'Do me a favor; come outside with me.' We went outside, and I took out the picture with Dayan and Dado to show him, asked him nicely to allow us to cross the canal; we had no problem getting permission.

When Rav Amital got to the other side, he visited with the troops, then asked for his son:

There was a cease-fire at the time. My son wanted to come home
to Israel for the wedding of a cousin. He had asked if he could go
to the wedding in one of the military planes. The officer he talked
to went to someone else and said: 'This soldier's cousin is getting
married and he needs to go to the wedding.' On that day, I arrived
and went to find my son. They told me he had gone to a wedding.
So I, a civilian, had to use *proteksia* – connections – just to visit
the troops on the other side of the canal, and my son, a combat
soldier, got released to go to a wedding with no *proteksia* at all.

Rav Amital's first contact with Rav Aharon Lichtenstein was by
letter. He had heard of him – "that he was a brilliant scholar, and a
man of great integrity."

I wrote him a letter and invited him to come as rosh yeshiva. I
didn't sign my name. He thought I was one of the workers here. I
was told I was crazy: 'What are you talking about. You can't have
two rosh yeshivas.' I told them we are a small yeshiva in tin buildings. You can't approach a rav on the level of Rav Lichtenstein and
just ask him to come. You have to offer him to be rosh yeshiva.
I am not worried about my own status. I went through the Holocaust; I should worry about getting along with a man like Rav
Lichtenstein? He came to talk. He saw what there was and agreed
to be rosh yeshiva along with me. We are from different worlds; I
am from Europe, he is from the United States. He is a Ph.D.; I had
four years of formal education before I entered the yeshiva.

Moshko was at first opposed to the idea of two *rashei yeshiva*. Rabbi Lichtenstein had at least two offers to become a *rosh
yeshiva*. Moshko was in favor of attracting him to Yeshivat Har
Etzion, but said: 'We already have a rosh yeshiva, and I am against
having two. Two kings can't wear the same crown. It won't work.
Rav Amital is a wonderful rosh yeshiva; we can't have two. Rav

Lichtenstein can come as the number two person.' I said, look, if we don't get along, it won't matter if I am the rosh yeshiva and he is *Sgan* – second-in-command. It simply wouldn't work. If we do get along, what does it matter if there are two *rashei yeshiva.'* Thirty years later we are doing fine.

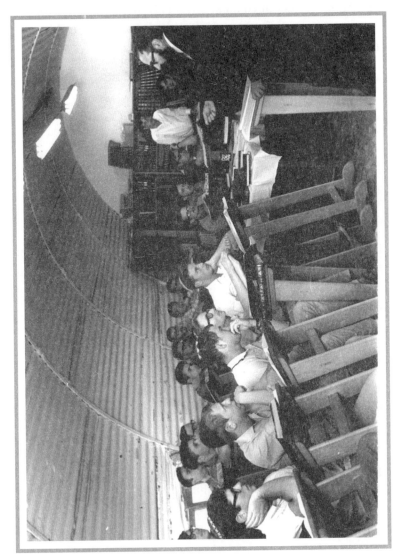

First Class, 1969. Yaacov Meidan is second from left, front row.

Chapter IV
The First Class

"**I** WANTED A YESHIVA with orientation toward greatness in Torah study. A yeshiva that combined this crucial characteristic with settlement on our historical land had great appeal," Rav Yaacov Meidan, explains in a soft, difficult-to-hear voice. "Rav Amital had such an orientation. Rav Kook's yeshiva, Mercaz HaRav was known for its Zionism, and some of the Gemarah teachers at other yeshivas would say that there was a choice: either you go to a yeshiva or you go to Mercaz – the clear implication being that Mercaz HaRav was not a "real" yeshiva. For me, this sentence made my decision.

"It is like the story of the respected rav who died and his students were not so sure that his son could carry on in the serious and profound manner in which his father had taught them. They came to speak with the son. He told them: 'Look, I am not sure if I can give you what you need. As there is nothing more important than your learning, I am going to leave, so you can learn from someone capable of leading you in the right path.' When the students heard this, they knew he had *ruach hakodesh* – the spirit of God, and they stayed with him."

Rav Meidan, a student in the first class of Yeshivat Har Etzion, describes the qualities of Rav Amital that drew him. "The ability to be self-reflective and self-critical is impressive and makes a big difference. Rav Amital projected a "quiet fire." The spirit of excellence in Torah is deep in him, but he did not try to impress on us, as prospective students, that studying in a *hesder* yeshiva in an isolated area was the only thing to do. He stated modestly what he thought he had to offer, and many were ready to follow him."

At the beginning of the Oslo process an event took place that, for Rav Meidan, illustrated the *gadlut* – greatness – of his rosh yeshiva. Rav Meidan was very disturbed about the proposal to give weapons to the Palestinian police, and decided to go on a hunger strike. Knowing that Rav Amital would not look kindly on the idea, Rav Meidan felt he must go to him and relate his plans. "Rav Amital was very angry, and told me so."

Rav Meidan proceeded with his plans and camped out opposite the Knesset. There was a great deal of publicity. Prime Minister Rabin was very angry about the publicity surrounding the hunger strike and called Rav Meidan into his office for a confrontation, to no avail. Visiting Rav Meidan more than once during the hunger strike was his rosh yeshiva, who disagreed with his tactics. Rav Meidan remembers: "When all of this was over, Rav Amital said to me, 'you did an important thing; you understand that someone who studies Torah, but does not hear the cry of a child, his study is faulty.'" Speaking to his students at the yeshiva after one of his visits to Rav Meidan, Rav Amital told them: "Although in principle I am against hunger strikes, and although Rav Meidan and I differ greatly in the political realm, I can't deny that I am proud that one of the first students of the yeshiva is carrying out the educational message that when a Jewish baby is crying, one must close the Gemarah and attend to the child's cry."

Rav Meidan was one of the leaders of those who stood on the rooftops of the small settlement of Yamit in 1978 when then Prime

Minister Menachem Begin acceded to Anwar Sadat's demand that the settlement be dismantled as part of the peace agreement between Israel and Egypt. "The idea of violence crossed our minds only to be certain that there would be none, and we communicated this to the police. We stayed to the bitter end; the police thanked us for our cooperation."

This scene repeated itself years later atop a hill near Efrat that was slated to be incorporated into the town as a new neighborhood. The Rabin government, in response to Arab complaints, withdrew permission for the settlement extension. Rav Meidan was again a leader of the protesters and again assured the police that there would be no violence among those demonstrating with him.

Two young men, not known to Rav Meidan and his group, began shouting radical slogans that Rav Meidan was concerned would incite violence. He suggested to the police that they remove the two demonstrators, but they decided not to do so. It was only later that the identity of the two became known: One was Avishai Raviv, the undercover Israeli secret service agent who, in many demonstrations, carried on such activity to discredit the opposition to the Oslo process. The other young man was Yigal Amir, the yeshiva student whom Raviv incited to murder Yitzhak Rabin.

Rav Meidan recalls another Rav Amital story about yet another son who succeeded his revered father as the head of his community. He changed some of the manner of teaching that had characterized his father. The students came to complain: "Why are you not carrying on in the tradition of your father," they wanted to know. Their new leader replied: "I *am* carrying on the tradition of my father. Like my father, who did not lead in the way his father had led his students, so too am I not leading in the way my father did."

Another anecdote told by Rav Amital very much influenced his students. The Rav of Kotsk spoke of three Jews who were thrown from heaven down to earth and told to climb back up to heaven. The first one tried and tried but ultimately gave up, as did the second.

The third man tried, and tried, and tried, and kept trying. Suddenly a ladder appeared, lowered from heaven.

A third tale that impressed Rav Meidan is one about the Rav of Kelme. He was teaching an important lesson about the "Song of Songs" when a man entered the room and began shouting something about his sick cow. Over and over he screamed. The Rav of Kelme stopped his lesson and related to the man with great seriousness. His students were incredulous: "How could you let this man interrupt such an important lesson?" The Rav said: "Oh, is that what you heard? You heard a disturbance? I heard that one of my community was asking for a relationship with his rav."

With these stories and his own personal example, Rav Amital deeply implants in his students the importance of the combination of Torah study and *derech eretz* – hearing the "cry of a child."

Rav Meidan is one of many examples of the cross-fertilization between the Har Etzion Yeshiva and the educational institutions of Efrat. He has felt, for a long time, that the educational gap between observant men and women is too large and this could pose the potential danger of losing religious women to non-religious men. He now has the opportunity to teach at Midreshet Lindenbaum, a Torah institute for women. He also teaches at Nishmat, a women's yeshiva where Rabbanit Hana Henkin has made history; four of her students were the first women in history to pass oral exams and receive certification by rabbinic authorities to be advisors in halachic issues pertaining to *taharat hamishpacha* – family purity.

Rav Meidan, along with Professor Ruth Gavison, was awarded the coveted Avichai Award for a report on how secular and religious Jews can work together to develop a common language on issues that divide them. Rav Meidan and Professor Gavison engaged in a two-year long dialogue on the issues between the religious and secular camps.

The report is entitled: "Foundation for a New Social Pact Between Religious and Secular Jews in Israel." Professor Gavison is a

Professor of Law at The Hebrew University and a senior fellow of the Israel Democracy Institute; a secular Jew, she found much in common with Rav Meidan who has published widely on religious issues. He is also a member of the board of the institution created, as a result of the Neeman Committee Report, to develop and supervise conversions under the auspices of Reform, Conservative, and Orthodox Jewish institutions.

So this is the man often branded by his opponents as a "radical." One might well call his activities an example of radical integrity – activities of a man who loves Eretz Yisrael and devotes enormous energy to bringing her people together.

Harav Aharon Lichtenstein

Chapter V
Rav Aharon Lichtenstein

IT WAS 1970, and Rav Aharon Lichtenstein, one of the foremost rabbinic scholars in the United States, was considering *aliyah*. He did not lack for offers in Israel. What drew him to Yeshivat Har Etzion, a yeshiva already headed by a very distinguished rosh yeshiva?

"First of all, it was the man next door," Rav Lichtenstein says, pointing to the nearby office of Rav Yehuda Amital. The love and respect between the two men is legendary. Never have two prominent rabbis shared the position of rosh yeshiva for thirty years. Rav Lichtenstein grows pensive as he describes their contact in 1970:

The sense which Rav Amital communicated was that he genuinely wanted me on board; there was a clear feeling that we could work together. He took me around and said: 'It is all yours. As much as you want to take, you can have.' I also got a tremendous sense of the spirit he had inculcated at Har Etzion. The boys were spirited and highly idealistic. But first and foremost, it was the people I would be working with. In that respect, Rav Amital's infectious warmth, his genuineness, made the difference more than anything else. I don't know if anyone realizes what a radical departure that was – to invite me in as rosh yeshiva. People don't usually do that, and certainly not people in the *yeshivishe* world. People who are in command want to remain in command. They don't invite someone else to share it with them. It was on his part a very generous move.

Tracing the background of Rav Lichtenstein, one begins to experience one of the subthemes that run through this book – that in the long sweep of history, the presence of the Jews in the United States will likely be seen as a transient phenomenon that peaked in the early to mid-twentieth century. By the end of the century, rampant assimilation, graphically charted by a series of demographic studies culminating in the major 1990 Jewish Population Study, appeared irreversible.

Rav Aharon Lichtenstein, like many Jews, passed through the United States on his way to Israel. He was born in Paris in 1933 to parents from very different backgrounds. His father, Dr. Yechiel Lichtenstein, was born in Kowal, a town in northwestern Poland not far from the German border. "He was subsequently raised and educated in Germany, first in Marburg, then in Würzburg," Rav Lichtenstein relates. "His Jewish education was centered in the German, *yekkishe* world. The college in Würzburg was a traditional teachers college for Jewish studies."

By contrast, Yechiel Lichtenstein's secular studies were heavily concentrated in the French language. His teaching and quest for additional learning took him to Switzerland where he taught at a finishing school run by a Dr. Ascher, a man who had a significant influence on his life. There he took great interest in French studies, especially from a Jewish aspect. Subsequently, he enrolled at the University of Neufchâtel in France where he was awarded a doctorate. The subject of his doctoral dissertation was "Racine as a Biblical Poet," a study that firmly established him in the French-speaking academic world.

Rav Lichtenstein's father was one of four children, all of whom survived World War II. His three siblings, one brother and two sisters, lived in Italy. In the mid-1930s, Mussolini expelled the Jews who did not have Italian citizenship. Mordechai and Devorah Lichtenstein, later Devorah Kinck, left for the United States, while Yehudit Lichtenstein, later Yehudit Grossman, immigrated to Israel. Rav Lichtenstein's parents and siblings escaped from France in December 1940 and arrived in the United States in January 1941.

In stark contrast to the German-Jewish, French-intellectual background of his father, Rav Lichtenstein's mother, Bluma Schwartz, was born in Telz, literally in the yard of the famous Telz Yeshiva. She received her early educational training primarily in Lithuania, where she attended the teacher's seminary in Kovno. An aunt and uncle were intensely involved in a group called Youth of Israel. Though the group was part of the yeshiva world, it encouraged a modern educational stream including secular subjects. As part of Bluma Schwartz's Jewish studies, there was an emphasis on the teaching of the Hebrew language.

Bluma Schwartz's parents, Rav Lichtenstein's maternal grandparents, had eleven children. Only his mother and five siblings lived to reach maturity. Of these six, one died of tuberculosis in the 1920s. One uncle died before World War II. Rav Lichtenstein's mother and one sister, Chana Ordman, survived the war and ultimately made their way to the United States, but three brothers were murdered in the Holocaust.

Rav Lichtenstein's early teachers were his parents. His father was an educator at the Maimonides School in Paris. Rav Lichtenstein characterizes the Paris school as "not strong in terms of the intensity of Jewish studies or in the intensity of *yirat shamayim* – reverence for God – by American standards, but it was very advanced compared to what they had in France before, which was just about zero."

His parents taught him reading, writing, and *chumash* – Bible –

in Paris until they fled, first from Paris to the countryside, then from Europe entirely, sailing to the United States. Rav Lichtenstein was seven years old, his older sister nine, and his younger sister five.

The family went to Baltimore where both parents were reunited with family. His father joined his brother Mordechai. One of his mother's uncles, Avraham Reichman Schwartz, was the Rabbi of Baltimore and had founded a Jewish school there. Rav Lichtenstein continued studying at home with his parents. The two years in Baltimore were very difficult economically, and when his father was offered a position in Chicago, the family moved.

In Chicago, Rav Lichtenstein studied at the Chicago Jewish Academy and received private tutoring as well. After two years, "it became clear that the type of education my parents wanted for their children was not available in Chicago," Rav Lichtenstein relates, "so, despite the financial difficulties of the move, in 1945 they settled in New York." There they stayed until they came on aliyah in 1972.

One of the major yeshiva high schools in New York was the Chaim Berlin Yeshiva, and Rav Lichtenstein studied there for four years. The revered Rav Isaac Hutner was the rosh yeshiva. Rav Hutner was born in Warsaw, Poland, where his reputation was established early as a child prodigy in Torah learning. He studied at the renowned Slobodka yeshiva that was founded in 1882 in Slobodka, a suburb of Kovno, Lithuania, and moved to Hebron in the 1920s when a branch of the yeshiva was established there. After many of his students were massacred by the Arabs in 1929, he returned to Europe. Rav Hutner moved to New York in 1935 in the shadow of the Nazi threat, and in 1939 he became head of the Chaim Berlin yeshiva.

At Chaim Berlin, some of Rav Lichtenstein's classmates dubbed him "Babe" Lichtenstein because of his rapid rise to the highest level of studies among whose students he looked like "a babe." In addition to Rav Hutner, a significant influence on Rav Lichtenstein was Rav Aaron Soloveitchik, the younger brother of Rav Joseph Dov

Soloveitchik, "the Rav." Rav Lichtenstein emphasizes Rav Aaron's tremendous influence on him as a high school student:

> He was a man of radical integrity. His level of personal honesty and consistency are at a level that is difficult not only to sustain, but even to envision. You felt that in his presence. It is something which cost him, because he was, in many respects, uncompromising. He was very congenial personally, but uncompromising when he thought an issue of principle was involved. In the practical world that can be a drawback, but in the ideal world, when you are looking for a person to emulate, he is a source of great inspiration.

WITH "THE RAV"

At Yeshiva University, Rav Lichtenstein entered the world of "the Rav." It is impossible to overestimate the influence of Joseph Dov Soloveitchik on two generations of American Orthodox rabbis. Born in Pruzhan, Poland, in 1903, he studied Talmud until his twenties, when he enrolled in the University of Berlin. There he entered the world of secular studies, culminating in a doctoral dissertation on the epistemology and metaphysics of Hermann Cohen. Rav Soloveitchik sailed for the United States in 1932 with his wife, Tonya, and became the spiritual leader of Boston's orthodox community.

In 1941, Rav Soloveitchik followed his father as professor of Talmud at the Isaac Elchanan Theological Seminary of Yeshiva University. In that role, and in his role as chairman of the Halachah Commission of the Rabbinical Council of America, Rav Soloveitchik exerted an unprecedented influence on American Jewry. When one speaks of "the Rav," there is no need to ask "which Rav."

Rav Lichtenstein was in Soloveitchik's *shir* – class – for the last of his three years of study at Yeshiva University. Rav Soloveitchik prevailed on his brilliant student to pursue a graduate degree at Harvard. Even though both of Rav Lichtenstein's parents had acquired higher levels of secular learning, such an education was not something that occurred to him to pursue:

> The Rav sold me on the idea of a higher degree in secular studies. He thought that, in conjunction with the world of Torah, a general education was very important. He himself had pursued that model. When he went for a higher degree, he could have gone to some second or third rate Polish or German university, but he went for the best, and the best at the time was Berlin. He thought I had the potential to combine the best of the Torah and secular worlds, and he encouraged me to do it. Whatever level I achieved, the Rav was several levels higher.

The greatest incentive for going to Harvard was the Rav's assurance that he would give private instruction to Rav Lichtenstein. The Rav learned with his family, thus he was giving his prized student a unique invitation to come into the inner circle of his family.

Rav Lichtenstein's secular studies opened up to him an entirely new world. While he excelled in his secular studies at Yeshiva University, there they had been "on a back burner." At Harvard, he was exposed to scholars who were masters in their field.

The Rav strongly encouraged Rav Lichtenstein to study mathematics, first at Yeshiva University and later at Harvard. "By way of accommodating him, I took two years of math in college, but I couldn't see myself devoting so much time to it." When it came to considering studies for a Ph.D., Rav Lichtenstein considered philosophy, but found it "too dry, too technical."

History was another option, but in the final analysis, Rav Lichtenstein chose literature "where both philosophy and history are interwoven as essential elements. I wanted something spiritual, and literature was more spiritual than history. At Harvard, my horizons were greatly expanded. I focused on the renaissance, but that encompassed more than just literature. I ended up essentially at the interface of philosophy and literature. That meant studying the French renaissance as well as the Italian renaissance."

Rav Lichtenstein's doctoral dissertation was on Henry Moore, a Christian religious humanist who was a contemporary of Isaac Newton. Rav Lichtenstein was drawn to Moore because he considers himself, like Moore, a religious humanist. The subtitle of his dissertation was "The Rational Theology of a Cambridge Platonist."

Harav Joseph Dov Soloveitchik
1903–1993

The Harvard period was "extremely intense, one in which I had virtually no contacts of any significance other than those which were related to my studies, or perhaps people I would see in Shul (Synagogue). Other than that it was total immersion. I would get home to New York for a Shabbos maybe every two or three months. It was a very stimulating period, one which I found helped develop me in many, many ways."

The word "studying" refers to secular subjects. "Learning," a word spoken with great respect, even reverence, refers to the world of Gemarah. While studying for his Ph.D., except during exam periods, Rav Lichtenstein was still able to learn Gemarah six hours a day:

> I had the enormous benefit of not just being in a class with the Rav, but experiencing him up close. That meant both the ability to cover more ground and also to be enriched by exposure to his personality. To be able to see how he worked things through and to be able to be involved in the chemistry of that directly, was a tremendous stimulus. I was stimulated to probe in directions

that would never occur to me if I were sitting by myself with a Gemarah.

A man as unique as Rav Soloveitchik and a relationship such as that between Rav Soloveitchik, the *melamed* (teacher) and Rav Lichtenstein, the *talmid* (student) is difficult to capture in words. Rav Lichtenstein struggles to give expression to the phenomenon:

> The Rav was an intellectual giant and a spiritual giant. In terms of what he communicated, that was very much part of his being. The man lived in a spiritual universe, one that most people not only don't live in, but a spiritual universe that most people are not even aware exists. It makes it difficult to define, but to him the notion of spirituality was a very important category. I remember he met once with one of the Rothschilds, a man who, in terms of religious observance, was totally removed. I asked him how the meeting went. He said: 'You know, he is a spiritual person.' And I knew that meant a great deal to him, even if it didn't translate into normative observance. These were not things that you necessarily saw on a day-to-day basis. But his religious and spiritual intensity was overwhelming.

Rav Lichtenstein first got to know his wife-to-be, Tovah, when he came into Rav Soloveitchik's home to study. Rav Soloveitchik invited favored students to come to his summer home on Cape Cod. At age nineteen, Rav Lichtenstein spent a month there with the Soloveitchik family. During the Harvard years, he was invited into the family circle where Rav Soloveitchik learned with his son, his daughters, and his son-in-law two hours every Friday evening and again two hours on Shabbat.

While there was no personal involvement between Rav Lichtenstein and his wife-to-be during those years, did the Rav see in his prize student a potential son-in-law? Rav Lichtenstein "never asked him, but people who knew him and knew me thought that this was part of his motivation."

There are similarities between Rav Soloveitchik and Rav Lichtenstein, not only in level of education and brilliance, but in personality. At Harvard, Rav Lichtenstein was almost totally engrossed in a private world of study, a world with few interpersonal relationships of any kind. He shares some of his insights into his own personality. "In the sense of being a part of a group that is advancing together in life, I envy those who have that. That is an element whose lacking in myself I deplore. I find myself, like the Rav, a bit of a loner. The reality is that there aren't too many people who have my combination of learning and interests. For example, I share a Zionist interest with people at Mercaz HaRav, but I don't share their ideology."

After acquiring his doctorate at Harvard, Rav Lichtenstein returned to New York in 1957. Though he had many offers from high-level academic institutions to teach in the field of English literature, he always knew he would return to the world of Torah.

Returning to New York, Rav Lichtenstein enjoyed the company of both his sisters who lived there at that time. His older sister, Shoshana, had earned a degree at Case Reserve in Cleveland, and was a social worker. Hadassah, the younger sister, studied at Brooklyn College and became a teacher. She was married in 1957, and moved to Israel in 1959, preceding her brother by twelve years. She teaches today at Horev High School in Jerusalem.

Rav Lichtenstein continued attending Rav Soloveitchik's *shir* in New York until he began teaching his own, highly sought-after *shir*. He taught at Stern College and served as an assistant to Rav Soloveitchik.

The four oldest Lichtenstein children, Moshe, Yitzhak, Meir and Esti were born in the United States. Shortly after the family came on *aliyah*, Shmuel was born. Tanya became the second Lichtenstein Sabra five years later.

Moshe Lichtenstein teaches at Yeshivat Har Etzion. Esti, Rabbanit Rosenberg, the oldest daughter, is the director of the Herzog College's women's yeshiva.

Zionism was a strong component of Rav Lichtenstein's upbringing. Hebrew was the language spoken in their home in Paris. He recalls that, already as a pre-teenager, he wanted to live in Israel. "I was a member of a youth group – *HaShomer HaDati*. I was young and impressionable, and my desire to come to Israel germinated there. I kept getting sidetracked." He traces his path from New York to Israel:

> The idea of moving to Israel remained latent. My first visit was in 1962. My wife was pregnant with our second child, so I came alone. I was able to crisscross the country. I came very much with the thought of eventually settling here. We might have come earlier, but my mother-in-law took ill with cancer in 1963, and that temporarily put everything aside. After she died, the Rav lived with his other daughter and son-in-law for twenty-six years, until his own death. An offer was made to me to come to Israel in 1968, but I couldn't think of leaving the Rav at that point. The next visit was in the winter of 1969–70 when my wife and I came. In the summer of 1970, we brought the whole family for two months.

That summer of 1970 was a critical one for Rav Lichtenstein. He was giving *shiurim* at Har Etzion and at Yeshivat Hakotel, which is the Yeshiva of the Western Wall. The yeshiva was established by Bnei Akiva, a religious-Zionist pioneering group established in 1929. After the Six-Day War in 1967, Bnei Akiva established the Yeshivat Hakotel near the Western Wall, and members of the movement were the first to resettle within the walls of the Old City of Jerusalem.

Rav Lichtenstein was facing not only the decision of when to come to Israel, but also what position to accept. All of the logical and pragmatic considerations favored Yeshivat Hakotel where he was asked to be rosh yeshiva. It was at the focal point of the Jewish world, the Western Wall in the center of the Old City of Jerusalem. Yeshivat Har Etzion was new and located in a wilderness. Yet the pull of the powerful personality of Rav Yehuda Amital and the inspired atmosphere of learning he had created at Yeshivat Har Etzion made the difference.

Rav Amital and Rav Lichtenstein share the same perception of their respective roles. There was never a time when they sat down to specify a division of duties. They each gravitated to areas that were their respective strengths. Hundreds of students and more than thirty years together testify to their success.

The chemistry between the two *Rashei Yeshiva* is captured well by Moshe Taragin who teaches at Yeshivat Har Etzion: "I think Rav Amital and Rav Lichtenstein do not see in their positions anything other than the opportunity to serve. Each one sees in the other those things that complement his own ability to contribute. This is reflected in the faculty as a whole. There is healthy disagreement, but no deviousness. That is possibly the greatest legacy of the yeshiva – focusing on the work to be done, the opportunity to serve, and less on personal issues. I think that those attitudes are carried with them by the students of this yeshiva even when they work in other organizations."

Rav Taragin speaks of Rav Lichtenstein with the great respect afforded to Rav Soloveitchik by Rav Lichtenstein:

In Rav Lichtenstein, the marriage of intellectual conquest with moral character is startling to me. The depth of his passion, the way he expresses his passions, the range of his character and the range of experiences on which that character was built – all are quite amazing. More than anything else, I guess, I am thankful for the manner in which he endowed me with depth of inner persona; he turned me from an artificial individual to someone capable of critical thinking, of deliberating before speaking. There are very few individuals in the world capable of endowing others with depth. You can endow knowledge and you can endow skill, you can convey information, but there are certain characters that touch you....He is a man of tremendous energy, one who draws energy and zeal from ideas – it is a mental energy of sorts, and I was overwhelmed by that at first. I try as much as possible in my life to emulate that quality.

Moshe Taragin grew up with brothers and had no girlfriends or friends who were girls. "You may be surprised," he says, "to hear that I chose a wife based on my yeshiva experiences. Here I saw very generous people who opened their homes to me. I have yet to be exposed to that selfless generosity elsewhere. For the first time I formed some sort of image as to who I wanted to marry, the family values that I wanted in my home."

Rav Taragin was married in the United States, after which the young couple moved to Israel in 1983. He is another example of the transient American Jewish experience. Both sets of grandparents came from Europe. His parents were born in America, yet Moshe and his two brothers are living in Israel. He and his wife have six children.

Despite the violence experienced in Israel in 2001–2002, there are still three applicants for every overseas student position at Yeshivat Har Etzion. Rav Taragin feels that the "intensity and commitment of the students is perhaps even highter than in previous years."

When asked to compare the intensity of study at Har Etzion to that experienced at a top secular university, Rav Taragin related what the father of one of his students told him: "When my son was in his high school yeshiva, he used twenty-five percent of his brain; at Harvard, he used fifty percent. At Yeshivat Har Etzion, he uses ninety-five percent."

Chapter VI
Efrat

THE ESTABLISHMENT of Yeshivat Har Etzion was a source of great satisfaction for Moshko, but those who know him well understand that he is not a man to rest on his laurels. In 1969, after Yeshivat Har Etzion was up and running, Moshko approached the government once again and told them he wanted to reestablish the ancient city of Efrat.

Yigal Alon, the government minister who helped Moshko pave the way for Alon Shevut and Yeshivat Har Etzion had passed away, so Moshko turned to Moshe Dayan who had also been involved in developing Alon Shevut. The first suggestion was put forward in 1969, the formal proposal presented in 1975, and the cornerstone laid in 1979. Moshko reflects: "This was a whole new concept. Who builds a city? The government. The government built Kiryat Arba, Maale Adumim, Neve Yaacov. I asked them to let me try. I told them: "I don't request anything more than you would invest in any city you establish; I promise you we will do better."

Just as Moshko had the wisdom to choose Yehuda Amital for the leadership of Yeshivat Har Etzion, he knew where to go for the religious educational leadership he envisioned for Efrat. "I don't know where I would be today if it were not for Moshko," Rav

Harav Shlomo Riskin

Shlomo Riskin reflects. "I had everything I could want in New York, at the Lincoln Square Synagogue. It's been a long journey."

A long journey indeed! Rav Riskin was born in Brooklyn in 1940 to a non-traditional Jewish family. His great-grandfather operated a factory in Brisk, Lithuania, that produced uniforms for the tsars. Working for him was his son, the grandfather of Rabbi Riskin. "My grandfather was a communist who truly believed in communism as an ideal. He organized the workers in the uniform factory against his own father."

Rabbi Riskin's grandfather was sent to Siberia, and from there made his way to New York, where he became a successful carpenter. Rabbi Riskin chuckles as he thinks about his grandfather: "There were two pictures on his wall. One was Stalin and the other was President Roosevelt. He felt Roosevelt was leading America towards socialism, then communism. I was very close to my grandfather. When I was a young kid, between the ages of eight and twelve, he and my father would at least make believe that they respected me as an adult. We would have real ideological debates. My grandfather knew *Yeshayahu – Isaiah –* by heart. He felt prophetic tradition was part of the socialist tradition. He had a real moral dilemma when I was Bar Mitzvah, because he had taken an oath at his own Bar Mitzvah that he would never again set foot in a synagogue."

His grandfather helped Rabbi Riskin work on his Bar Mitzvah speech that was delivered in Yiddish and lasted more than an hour. He helped, but kept saying he didn't know if he would be able to come. "I didn't know until the last minute whether or not he would show up," Rabbi Riskin remembers. His grandfather compromised with himself and showed up in the middle of the Bar Mitzvah service with a brown paper bag in which were two books, his gifts to his grandson; one was *Das Kapital* and the other was *The Communist Manifesto*.

By contrast, Rabbi Riskin's maternal grandparents were deeply religious, in particular his grandmother. They both came to

America from Lubien, a small town on the Slovak border of Poland. Her father was Rav Shlomo Kowalsky, the *dayan* (judge) of that town. According to family legend, he lived to be 115 years old. In the course of time he had three wives. Rabbi Riskin's grandmother was the first child of his first wife, followed by three more girls.

Rav Kowalsky was a *talmid chacham* who gave regular lessons to his daughters, including Gemarah. Rav Riskin's grandmother *davened* (prayed) three times a day. She had seven children, not one of whom was religious in adulthood. Thus it was in that part of the world at the time; many people wanted to Americanize. Rabbi Riskin's mother was the seventh and youngest child. Warm memories of his grandmother are constantly with Rav Riskin. "When I was eight years old, my grandfather got very sick. He had a stroke. I spent every Friday evening with my grandmother. I watched her *bentsh licht* – light candles. She would mention every child, grandchild, great-grandchild, and talk to God. I saw her literally talking to God. We sang *zmirot* (Shabbat melodies) together. We studied Torah and Talmud together."

When Rav Riskin's grandmother, Chaya Beila Walters, left Europe, she asked her father for a picture of himself. He would not have his picture taken, so instead he gave her a *Shas* – a complete set of the six tractates of the Gemarah. When she finished studying with her grandson the tractate on *brachot* (blessings), she gave the set of Gemarah to him.

Rav Riskin's own parents were not religious. They went to synagogue on the high holy days and went to a Passover Seder at his grandmother's house; this was the limit of their observance. They sent their son to a Jewish Day School, not for religious reasons, but because they considered the quality of education to be higher than that in the public schools. Rav Riskin relates: "The day school was a yeshiva in Brooklyn. Rav Menachem Mandel was the head of the school. He was a very warm, loving and kind principal. He came from Yeshiva Torah Vadaath. He took me to his home, a mile or two away, every *Shabbat* for lunch. Those were formative experiences in my growing up, and they were definitely my deepest and most profound religious influences."

While still living at home, Rav Riskin became Torah observant, as did his two sisters. One sister eventually joined a Conservative synagogue. "She is a bit more religious than my parents," Rav Riskin adds. His youngest sister retained her Orthodox life style, and now lives next door to her brother, in Efrat. She has seven children.

Rav Riskin wanted to go to a yeshiva high school, but his parents were very much against it. They wanted him to become a lawyer. When it was time for college, Rav Riskin still was not drawn to a career in law, despite the fact that he was granted a full scholarship to Harvard. He recalls the turning point:

> On Shavuot, I went to the main campus of Yeshiva University, because they had learning all night. I had a wonderful night. There was a full *beit midrash* – religious study hall. I was extremely impressed. There was davening. I remember Rav Lessin. He was tall, with an immaculate white beard, extremely well kept. He wore a black cutaway and was very impressive. He came at dawn and led us in singing. He had a Lavotka *nigun* (tune) that was beautiful. Near Yeshiva University lived a great-aunt. She was not observant, but we became very close. One day, she took me in tow and marched me, without an appointment, into the office of Dr. Samuel Belkin – the president of Yeshiva University. She said, 'this is my great-nephew, my sister is his grandmother, and he should have a scholarship.' Rav Lessin was very warm, gave me a test, and I went to Yeshiva University on full scholarship for four years.

At Yeshiva University, Rav Riskin began studying Latin, because Rabbi Isaac Luria's works were written in Latin. He was very much drawn to the Professor of Latin, Louis Feldman. "He was a wonderful scholar in the classics. He was young, but a very tough teacher, very intellectually driven and intellectually honest." Rav Riskin majored in Greek and the Classics, taking every course Professor Feldman offered.

In his sophomore year, Rav Riskin had a transforming experience, one he shares with Rav Aharon Lichtenstein and hundreds of other graduates of Yeshiva University; he had the opportunity to study with Rav Soloveitchik: "It changed my life. I realized from him how alive the Gemarah can be." Rav Riskin struggles to adequately describe the experience:

> It is almost impossible to reproduce what a class was like. When he walked in, everyone was on the edge of his seat. The Rav was very demanding. He had everything at his fingertips. He asked questions and interpretations. If you didn't know, he got very upset, and would sometimes kick you out. There was tremendous tension. You never ate before his class, because you were too nervous. My stomach always settled on Thursday when the Rav was on his way back to Boston. But no one could bring alive the Gemarah like the Rav. He made you look at a page of the Talmud and made you understand that whatever you had seen had nothing to do with what it was actually saying. He would begin reading and opened up a live world for us. It was as if the Rambam walked into the class for his commentary, and the Vilna Gaon. It was a kind of living drama that has never been duplicated for me anywhere.

Rav Riskin recalls an incident that illustrates a harsher side of the Rav, and at the same time, his high level of integrity:

> I had a friend that I encouraged to transfer into the Rav's class. He sat in the back, because most people were intimidated by the Rav and did not want to be close. I always sat up front. I felt I

would rather take the blows and take in as much as I could get. I encouraged my friend, Horowitz, to move up a row every week, and he did, finally sitting right behind me. Horowitz whispered to me that he had a question and wanted me to ask it. I told him to ask the question, and he did. Rav Soloveitchik was right in the middle of one of his amazing explanations and did not appreciate being interrupted. The Rav said: 'You are one of Riskin's friends. I never should have let you into this class.' The poor guy was devastated, and I was devastated. The Rav taught a second class just after that class, and I was in both. At the beginning of the second class, the Rav sat up front, lost in thought. No one made a sound. After twenty minutes of absolute silence, he turns to me and says: 'Riskin, your friend who asked the question at the end of the last class, what's his name?' I said his name is Horowitz. 'Take me to him.'

Rav Soloveitchik rose and left the classroom with Rav Riskin following close behind.

The Rav had a brisk gait that was very distinct. We walked to a restaurant across the street – we used to call it "the greasy spoon" – where I thought we would find Horowitz. There he was sitting alone at a table, the color just beginning to return to his face after what happened in class. The Rav had never come into the restaurant before. Horowitz stood up, shocked, and everyone in the place stood up. The Rav walked up to Horowitz and said: 'Horowitz, you were right, and I was wrong. I have to rethink everything.' He then walked out and went back to give his second class.

After college, Rav Riskin decided to study in Israel. It was for him "one of those never to be forgotten experiences." He took courses in many different places, soaking up all the learning that the land of Israel had to offer. He studied Gemarah, and philosophy. He took courses on Gershom Scholem and Shabtai Tzvi. He had no money, so he took an offer from Yeshiva University to stay at the Chaim Blumberg Institute in the Baka neighborhood of Jerusalem. He received a small stipend for serving as a counselor to both the boys and the girls at the co-educational institute. One of the instructors there was the renowned Nehama Leibowitz. These were for him extremely rich experiences.

At the end of these classes, Rav Riskin decided to taste kibbutz life and went to Kibbutz Sha'alvim. He also studied at Kerem Beyavne, the only *hesder* yeshiva in Israel at the time. There he learned with Rav Goldwicht and began to study the works of Rav Kook. "I studied the whole world of Rav Kook, his writings, his philosophy, his Zionism. That was when I pretty much decided I would live in Israel."

His Israeli reverie was interrupted by a telegram from Yeshiva University inviting him to join its first *kollel*. He had missed being in Rav Soloveitchik's *shiur*, so returned to New York, staying in the *kollel* for two years. Every Shabbat he and a friend went to a different community to do *kiruv* – teaching in order to draw Jews closer to their religion. He was paired with a fellow kollel member, Mickey Posnick. They went to many communities and many synagogues. In Conservative synagogues they would put up a *mechitzah* – a divider between the men's and women's praying areas. Rav Riskin loved to teach and was good at it. "Mickey had a great voice. He sang, and I did most of the talking."

His love affair with Israel was renewed when he was a counselor on a summer trip with Yeshiva University's Synagogue Council of Youth. There he met Vicki, his wife to be. Rav Riskin loves to talk about his and Vicki's background and their long love affair:

> My wife comes from a totally assimilated family, more assimilated even than mine. Her family is six generations in America, and the rumor is that her great-grandmother fasted on Yom Kippur. After that generation, no one even knew there was such a thing as Yom Kippur. My wife's family lived in Queens, and they had

never seen the inside of a Shul. My wife was very bright, and her parents sent her to the United Nations school, an excellent school. When she was fourteen years old, there was a school trip to Europe. She went, and the trip included Germany, where she learned about the Holocaust. When she returned, she told her parents she wanted to go to Israel. Her mother knew about a large synagogue in Queens, so thought it was a good place to learn about trips to Israel. When she asked the executive director about her daughter joining a youth trip to Israel, the director asked if her daughter was observant. My mother-in-law understood the question to be: 'Does your daughter observe things well?' She answered affirmatively: 'My daughter is extremely observant.'

For the two young people, it was love at first sight. Since she attended Barnard College, Rabbi Riskin assumed Vicki was eighteen – "she was very mature." In fact, she was only sixteen years old. They wanted to get married right away, even though Rav Riskin had no prospects of a job. "My in-laws were devastated," Rav Riskin relates. "They thought their daughter's Orthodoxy was a passing phase. Here is a guy who wants to be an Orthodox rabbi wanting to take away their sixteen year-old daughter. Her father would leave the room when I came into the house." Her parents insisted their daughter see a psychiatrist.

Rav Riskin suggested they go to see the psychiatrist together. "They paid for us to see a psychiatrist named Dr. Careys. We had two sessions with him, and he reported that these were the two most mature young people he had ever met in his life and, as far as he was concerned, we should get married."

The marriage took place two years later, in 1963, when Rav Riskin received *smicha* – rabbinical ordination. Rav Riskin's relationship with his in-laws changed drastically. "The relationship became very close. They became like my own parents."

Soon after he was married, Rav Riskin was approached by Rav

Moshe Besdin who was in charge of the Jewish studies program at Yeshiva University, the James Striar School. Most of the students were young men with little or no yeshiva background. Rav Besdin had heard Rav Riskin speak and wanted him on his faculty. Thus, Rav Riskin became an assistant professor at Yeshiva University at age twenty-three.

On Sunday mornings, he taught at the Hebrew High School in Queens. "My wife became pregnant right away, but we made ends meet." Rav Riskin has only the fondest memories of his time on Rav Besdin's staff. "We became very close. A few times a week we would take two-hour lunches and talk. Any question I had on teaching methodology, I would ask him. He knew a great deal."

In the 1960s, Yeshiva University had a program called *Kibbush Kehilot* – to conquer congregations. They worked with congregations that had few resources. Those congregations that did not have a *mechitzah* would be put under the Yeshiva University aegis on a trial basis, with the understanding that the congregation might want to become traditional.

It was clear to Rabbi Riskin that he would not work in a congregation that did not have a *mechitzah*. When Yeshiva University received a request from a Conservative congregation in Lincoln Square that someone come to meet with them about their needs, Rav Riskin was asked to go. Lincoln Square, the area that was the setting of *West Side Story*, was one of the first older New York areas to be gentrified. The city opened a Lincoln Center of the Performing Arts, including a cultural center and an opera house. Expensive apartments were constructed.

There was a Conservative congregation in the neighborhood that held services only on the High Holy Days. A rabbi who organized men's clubs for the Conservative Movement's Jewish Theological Seminary functioned there during rosh Hashanah and Yom Kippur. Some members wanted to have a Shabbat service between the two High Holy Days, while others did not. The first group wanted to interview a rabbi connected with Yeshiva University. Others objected to anything connected with Orthodoxy. After a serious argument, they agreed at least to interview someone from Yeshiva University. Rav Riskin consented to speak with them and evaluate their needs.

After a three-hour meeting, the leaders of the congregation said they wanted Rav Riskin to be their Rabbi. He thanked them for their interest, but insisted he would not serve a congregation with mixed seating. The leaders were not ready to make that change, but urged Rav Riskin to take the position. The more he said no, the more adamant they became.

Rav Riskin decided to consult Rav Soloveitchik, who advised him that the chances the congregation would put in a *mechitzah* were slim, and that going there would hurt his reputation. Rav Soloveitchik offered to help him find a suitable congregation. So that was the end of the story – or so it seemed. Rav Riskin recalls what happened next:

> I received a call from Dr. Belkin, the president of Yeshiva University, to come see him. He had maintained a relationship with me and we liked one another. He suggested I take the shul. I didn't know the pecking order, the hierarchy; I was very naïve about all of that. So I said to him that my rosh yeshiva told me not to take it. He got very angry and reminded me that he was the rosh yeshiva. Then he dug his nails into the desk and said with irony: 'Okay, fine, tomorrow your rosh yeshiva will tell you to take the congregation.' And the next day I received a call from Rav Soloveitchik. I went to see him, and he told me that he had never told me that it was forbidden for me to go, from the point of view of *halachah*. He had only said that he though it inadvisable: 'But Dr. Belkin knows the neighborhood very well, he knows you, and he feels you would be able, in a reasonable time, to convince them to put up a mechitzah. I would say, go, give it a two year trial.'

Rav Riskin was torn and slept little that night. His wife suggested he consult with the Lubavitcher Rebbe. "I had nothing to do with the Lubavitcher Rebbe, but this was the early 1960s. He was available, and he understood the whole Jewish community. So I went to see him, and I was very impressed. He told me: 'In Rav Soloveitchik, you have a Rav of great stature. You should always listen to him.'

Bucking the trend at the time of Orthodox shuls turning Conservative, the Conservative Lincoln Square Synagogue became Orthodox in a very short period. At the beginning of Rav Riskin's tenure, there were twenty to thirty members, none of them *shomer Shabbat* – Sabbath observant. Shabbat services were held with a *mechitzah*. In the nineteen years Rav Riskin served at Lincoln Square, the development was dramatic. The synagogue became a dynamic center of learning, with many outreach programs.

A beginners *minyan* – worship service of at least ten men – was instituted for people with little Jewish knowledge. Many classes were taught, from the lowest level to advanced Talmud classes. An elementary school called Ohr Torah was opened, followed by an Ohr Torah high school for boys and girls.

In February 1975, Rav Riskin was one of five American rabbis asked to participate in a conference organized by the religious kibbutz movement. Each rabbi was then assigned to be a scholar-in-residence at a kibbutz, Rav Riskin's kibbutz being Ein Tzurim. Ein Tzurim was one of the four original settlements in Gush Etzion before they fell in 1948 to the Arabs. After the 1948 War of Independence, Ein Tzurim was reestablished near Ashkelon.

At Ein Tzurim he was the guest of Zahava and Yehuda Noimann. Rav Riskin describes Noimann as a quiet, unassuming *talmid chacham* whose father was "a very great *talmid chacham* from Kfar Saba. Anyone who had a question about Jewish philosophy or *halachah* would call him. He knew the whole Jewish world. And his son, Yehuda, was very much like him." After that first visit to

Ein Tzurim, Rav Riskin was invited back as a scholar-in-residence every summer from 1975 until 1983, when he moved to Efrat.

"I didn't know anything about the early Zionists. Yehuda Noimann took me to the Gush and told me the whole history. Through him, I fell in love with the Gush." In 1976, Moshko said to me: "What are you doing in America? We need you in Israel." I said I had dreams of teaching in Israel. Moshko took Rav Riskin in a car to "this empty hill which was Efrat." Moshko told him the story of Dizengoff, the first mayor of Tel Aviv, who was asked: "How do you become the mayor of a city?" Dizengoff said, "If you want to become mayor of a city, build yourself a city."

Moshko stood on that empty hill with Rav Riskin and said: "Come, be my partner in building the city of Efrat. Remember that the Old City of Jerusalem fell right after Gush Etzion fell. Gush Etzion, overlooking Jerusalem, is two hundred and fifty meters higher than the Holy City. The future of Jerusalem is indelibly bound up with the future of Gush Etzion. Let's make the dream come true; I will be the mayor and you will be the rabbi." The two men shook hands and vowed to make the dream a reality.

It took from 1976 until 1981 to get permission to go ahead with the project. Twice during that period, Rav Riskin asked then Israeli ambassador to the United States, Yitzhak Rabin, to speak at his Lincoln Square synagogue. "He was not a man to get excited," Rav Riskin says, "but he spoke with a great deal of emotion about Gush Etzion, of the building of Efrat. He was extremely positive and said everyone should follow Rabbi Riskin to Efrat. It would always be an integral part of Eretz Yisrael."

The laying of the cornerstone for Efrat in 1981 was preceded by many delays, the most frustrating of which was overcome only by the tenacity of Moshko and Rav Riskin – the two men who lived the dream of Efrat.

The night of Rav Riskin's flight to Israel for the groundbreaking, he performed a wedding in Queens. It was the thirty-year anniversary of Rabbi Menachem Mendel Schneerson's becoming the head of the Lubavitch Movement. Rav Riskin was invited, but said he would have to be late due to the wedding. "When I arrived, my Rav, Rav Soloveitchik, was just leaving, and they sat me in his place up front. I had been trying to see the Rebbe to get his *bracha* – blessing for Efrat. Rabbis Krinsky and Groner, the Rebbe's top assistants, had mentioned that there might be an opportunity that night."

In the early morning hours, the Rebbe finished speaking and got up to leave the hall. When he reached Rav Riskin's place, he stopped and said, in yiddish: "Rabbi Riskin, the Rebbe has you in his prayers." Rav Riskin asked the Rebbe for a blessing for Efrat, and the Rebbe said once, then twice: "God will grant you success." Rav Riskin says, "Look, I'm not a chassid. My Rav is Rav Soloveitchik, but I was overwhelmed. I took the plane to Israel with extra wings."

When Rav Riskin landed in Israel, he was met by Moshko. "There is not going to be a cornerstone laying ceremony," he said. There had been a violent incident in Hebron and the government had decided to cancel all activities in the Gush. The two men agreed they needed the momentum of the ceremony; they had to do something. The only man who could reverse the decision of the government was the prime minister, Menachem Begin. Moshko turned to Rav Haim Druckman, a minister in the government close to Begin. Begin agreed to let the ceremony go forward, with the proviso that there would be no publicity. Despite its absence, the word spread and a very large crowd was on hand for the festive proceedings.

Rav Riskin had all the essential credentials to be a rabbi in Israel, but in order to serve as rabbi of a city, he had to pass a special test. When he submitted his application to take the examination, he ran into the infamous Israeli bureaucracy. He was told he might as well not take the exam, because he had two strikes against him: he did not have a beard, and his daughter had done army service – not a badge of honor among the *charedim*. He persisted but was told a canditate was required to have published. He told them he had publications to his credit. "But in *halachah* – Jewish law – have you published?" Again, Rav Riskin answered yes, a whole book on *halachah*. "But in Hebrew?" Since the answer was negative, he was told to translate his book into Hebrew and then come back.

Rabbi Riskin turned to the Ashkenazi Chief Rabbi, Rav Avraham Shapira. Rav Shapira made a few phone calls and said: "They will give you an oral exam. I cannot tell you whether or not you will pass, but you can take the examination." Rabbi Riskin showed up at the appointed time, 8:30 AM. First, the three-man panel of rabbis who were to administer the exam were late, and, when they arrived, other candidates were called, one after the other, but not Rav Riskin.

Rav Riskin went to Rav Shapira's office and sought help. Again he picked up the phone. "What about Riskin?" he asked. "The one without the beard? We aren't testing him," was the answer. Rav Shapira insisted that Rav Riskin have the opportunity to be examined. So at 1:15 PM, "nervous, with my ego blasted to smithereens and having had no lunch," he was finally called in for the examination. "The atmosphere was so thick, you could have cut it with a knife," Rav Riskin recalls. The three rabbis began questioning him with "not so difficult questions, but I knew they could find hard questions – it's a big Gemarah and there are thousands of difficult issues."

Finally, the difficult question came; it was a question about a woman who wanted to divorce her husband because she found him distasteful. Unbeknownst to the judges, Rav Riskin had written a book on the subject. Moreover, he had written of a case in which one of his examiners, Rav Shaul Yisraeli, was involved; Rav Yisraeli's position was rejected in the actual case. However, in his own research for the book, Rav Riskin found a responsum in the Cairo Geniza that supported Rav Yisraeli's position. So, after giving his examiners a twenty-minute discourse on the subject, Rav Riskin closed by citing the Cairo Geniza and said directly to Rav Yisraeli: "You were one-hundred per cent correct!"

Rav Riskin passed the examination and became the Chief Rabbi of Efrat.

Morton Landowne of New York was intimately involved in the development of Lincoln Square Synagogue, He first met Rav Riskin in 1961. "It was at a *shabbaton* sponsored by Yeshiva University. Subsequently, I was invited to attend a Torah leadership seminar conducted by the university. These were programs to reach out to those high school students, like myself, who did not attend a yeshiva, but were affiliated with synagogue youth groups." Mort attended the seminars twice a year through the decade of the 1960s, first as a student, then as a staff member, starting in 1965, when he began his studies at Yeshiva University.

In 1964, Rav Riskin and his wife Vicki were the leaders of the Yeshiva University summer trip to Israel, and Mort was one of the participants. "That is when I really got to know them very well." At Yeshiva University, Mort was a student in the Jewish Studies Program, "sort of a first *baal tshuva* yeshiva." He often spent Shabbat with the Riskins at the time.

It was Yom Kippur 1964, when Rav Riskin first came to Lincoln Square. In 1970, Mort graduated with a B.A., married his wife Rose, and joined Lincoln Square Synagogue. This was the last year of the synagogue's location in a Lincoln Towers apartment. "I remember it being a very exciting place. There we were in that apartment that held maybe a hundred or a hundred and thirty people, and we were building this shul that would seat five hundred. The first week the new shul was open, it was full. It was astonishing – we went from 130 to 500; the minute more space was available, it was filled." Mort makes clear the reason for the success:

> Rabbi Riskin was the catalyst – he personally. The growth of the
> West Side as a real mecca for Jews, and a place that is so welcom-

ing and comfortable for Jews to live, all of this was because of Rabbi Riskin. The growth of Lincoln Square led to the Drisha Institute. Rabbi Riskin started a yeshiva and hired David Silber. Effie Buchwald worked for Lincoln Square as outreach director, and that led to him starting the national Jewish outreach program. Rabbi Riskin set the standard nationally for a rabbi serving his congregation, doing outreach, and relating to Israel.

What is it about Rabbi Riskin? How is he able to have this enormous influence?

He is a very, very caring, authentically warm individual. He conveys that one on one, and he conveys it when he speaks to five hundred people. He has this God-given ability to connect with people on their level. He has this infectious enthusiasm that draws people in. I know him very, very well, and the better you know him, the more you realize how sincere he is. There was a fellow who showed up at the synagogue. I was introduced to him. His father was a well-known actor. In fact, his father specialized in playing Jewish roles. His name was Joe Silver. He was in the movie Dudie Kravitz as Dudie Kravitz's father. He was on Broadway. He had intermarried. In fact his wife, I think, was the longest playing "Golda" in *Fiddler on the Roof* on Broadway, even though she wasn't Jewish. They had a son named Christopher Silver, who was not Jewish. He was traveling in Germany and found himself in a Chabad House and became interested in Judaism. He showed up at Lincoln Square. He had written a novel, and Rabbi Riskin took the time to read the manuscript and encourage him. This is the perfect example of how Rabbi Riskin relates to people at whatever level, takes the time to show them he cares about them. So now Christopher Silver is Moshe Silver and has converted to Judaism. Multiply this by hundreds of stories, and you see the impact Rabbi Riskin has had.

Another person to whom Rabbi Riskin responded positively became one of his strongest financial supporters. Sanford Bernstein was an extremely successful, self-made man who popularized the concept of personalized money management for people who were not the super-rich. His company gave them the personal care and expert money management usually reserved for the financial elite. Bernstein was intermarried and had two children. When his father died in the 1970s, he went into a synagogue on the east side of New York, requesting to join and say *kaddish* for his father. The synagogue would not let him join, because his wife was not Jewish. Mort Landowne describes how Bernstein met Rabbi Riskin:

> Sanford Bernstein had a friend named Jerry Stern, someone in whose life Rabbi Riskin has also played a major part. Jerry invited Sanford to start coming to the Wednesday night lectures at Lincoln Square Synagogue, and he did come. He met Rabbi Riskin and they formed a good relationship. Sanford changed his name to Zalman and started the Avichai Foundation. The foundation became a mainstay of support for Rabbi Riskin. It was a two-way relationship. The two of them dreamed together of what could be done. Today, the Avichai Foundation has enormous resources and is doing wonderful work in Israel and really all over the world. All of this began with Rabbi Riskin being open to the religious needs of one man by welcoming him to say Kaddish for his father.

At the height of his success at Lincoln Square, Rabbi Riskin, a deeply believing religious Zionist, responded to Moshko's call to take the risk of starting all over from scratch on a series of rocky hills outside of Jerusalem. Mort recalls that, not too long after Rabbi Riskin made *aliyah*, he was visiting Lincoln Square and what was billed as a debate took place between Rabbi Berl Wein and Rabbi Riskin. The question was whether an American rabbi should make *aliyah*. Rabbi Wein, who did not make *aliyah* until some years later, took the position that an American rabbi's skills were not suited to Israel and he should serve his congregation in America. I don't know if he really believed that, but the discussion made for an entertaining evening. Rabbi Riskin responded that he had taken the risk to move to Israel and that it was working out well. Rabbi Wein quipped back: "With all due respect, Rabbi Riskin, you would be successful if you moved to the moon."

Mort Landowne points out that Rabbi Riskin provides significant continuity to the tradition of "The Rav." "Rav Aharon – Aharon Lichtenstein – is the model of the scholar that the Rav produced, and it is clear that Rabbi Riskin is the model of the congregational rabbi and Jewish leader that the Rav produced; this was an important part of Rav Soloveitchik's legacy."

Rabbi Riskin began talking about the idea of building Efrat a number of years before he made *aliyah*. He formed an organization called *Reishit Geula* – the Beginning of Redemption." Close to one hundred people put down a five thousand dollar deposit toward settling in Efrat. Mort estimates that a large percentage of those people made *aliyah*, though "many did not wait for Efrat. It seemed like forever. There is the wonderful story of his mother-in-law who went to the site and called Rabbi Riskin's mother and told her not to worry. 'It's just a hill with a bunch of rocks. Not in your lifetime or in my lifetime will it be built.' Yet, once Moshko got all the permits, it developed rapidly."

Rav Riskin's departure from Lincoln Square ended an unusual eighteen-year partnership between him and Cantor Sherwood Goffin. Cantor Goffin had been headed in an entirely different direction: "Originally I wanted to be a psychologist. I wanted to work as a cantor on the High Holy Days, perhaps. Then Rabbi Riskin called me when I was in the middle of psychology grad school and talked me into trying out for the job at his shul. He convinced me to change the direction of my life for the last eighteen years."

In a newspaper interview at the time, Cantor Goffin expressed his feelings as he approached a final concert before Rav Riskin left for Efrat: "It's an emotional time. This whole year has had a bittersweet feeling. Every time I do something, it's our last time doing it together – our last community seder, our last Sukkot, our last Shavuot. Its been a very difficult year. And, when I sing on Wednesday, I'm going to be giving it everything I've got to give the rabbi a great send off."

Lincoln Square Synagogue gave Rabbi Riskin a one-year leave of absence, hoping against hope that he would return. The synagogue engaged an acting rabbi. Half-way through the year, Rabbi Riskin let them know that his move to Efrat was permanent. Mort relates that Rabbi Riskin was a realist about the assimilation in the United States; he did not foresee an improvement in the situation. He believed that part of being a modern Orthodox Jew was being serious about living in Israel.

While Mort and his wife Rose, who was among the founders of the Lincoln Square Synagogue nursery school and ran it for many years, still live in New York, it is clear that theirs is a family with roots in Europe which will stop over in the United States for a few generations before ending up in Israel. They already own an apartment in Jerusalem and visit frequently. Their eldest daughter, Dena, is married and living in Efrat. She and her husband, Jay Bailey, have one son and one daughter. Lea, their second born made *aliyah* in 2002, and Shifra, the youngest of the daughters is studying in Rabbi Riskin's Midreshet Lindenbaum in Jerusalem. Aryeh, the youngest child and only son, is still in college. "I am sure we will all end up in Israel," Mort asserts.

Vicki Riskin, a colorful, dynamic driving force alongside her husband, has many memories of the transition from Lincoln Square to Efrat, some of them positive and others not so pleasant. She recalls fondly Moshko's visits to New York. "We took him to H&H Bagels at midnight on Saturday night. He couldn't believe there was

Jewish life so late at night. He was inspiring in his vision, but always modest, self-effacing." Once groundbreaking took place in Efrat in 1979, "we called Moshko every week for an update. Moshko sent pictures and we shared the excitement of the unfolding adventure."

Rav Riskin began speaking to his congregation about Efrat as early as 1980, feeling he was making it clear that this was his future. Vicki recalls the Purim party in 1983 when she made costumes. She and Rav Riskin came dressed as an El Al airline pilot and stewardess. One congregant said to them: "Oh what are you, a couple from Borough Park?" Vicki remembers the transition from Lincoln Square to Efrat as a traumatic process:

> Some members didn't get it; they didn't want to get it. We were in the middle of a cultural maelstrom – everything was changing at a rapid pace. There were power walks, power lunches, power everything. Lincoln Square was a refuge for all of us; no one wanted it to change. The idea that their rabbi would leave was too painful to think about. Before we left, Zalman Bernstein made a going away party at his home in Pound Ridge, Connecticut. There were 80-100 people. Other than when something tragic happens, that was the worst day of my life. The congregation had arranged for a Sefer Torah to be written, inscribed 'To our Rebbe.' It was such a painful parting.

Vicki is the only descendant on her father's side who is religious. Her father, the second child of his parents, was the only son. He had three sisters. On that side of her familly, all of Vicki's first cousins married Jews, but none of their children did so. "One cousin is profoundly anti-religious."

Vicki's mother's side is characterized by rampant assimilation, except for one of her mother's first cousins who married a Yeshiva University graduate. "The family was rife with Christmas trees, wreaths, people being cremated – the whole bit."

Vicki's own family continues to grow in Israel. She and Rabbi Riskin have four children, Batya, Ilana, Hillel and Yona, all married, with growing families.

EDUCATIONAL INSTITUTIONS

Rav Riskin has established an impressive number of high quality educational institutions. Many of them are staffed by graduates of Yeshivat Har Etzion. Heading the yeshiva high school in Efrat is Rav Yaacov Fischer, a graduate of the third class of Har Etzion and a resident of Alon Shevut. He also serves on the board of Yeshivat Har Etzion.

As Rav Fischer speaks, one feels the strength of his attachment to Gush Etzion; indeed it is part of his soul. Both of his parents are *nitzulei shoah* – survivors of the Holocaust – and the Gush symbolizes for him the renewal of the Jewish people. "To live here, right on the land where *Avraham avinu* walked, along the very route on which he led Isaac to the *akedah*, to be this close to Jerusalem, Jerusalem that was in the hearts and souls of our forefathers, it is as if I have come to live in a place where, in fact, I have always been."

It was this same depth of emotion he sensed in Moshko and Rav Amital when he first came to Yeshivat Har Etzion.

> This place established them, gave life to them, and they came back after the 1967 war to establish and give life to the place. They had strong roots in the past, in the ground; they had aspirations and dreams, but not only that; they were determined to make those things real and they did. To study there and watch them build the place, piece by piece, day by day, hour by hour, is something tremendous. It had a great pull on me as someone whose family also has strong roots in the past and suffered so much in the *Shoah*. From time to time, I tell my students of the feeling I have when I ask myself: What would my grandfather think – my grandfather who was murdered in Auschwitz – to know that his

grandson is a rosh yeshiva in Gush Etzion, that he studies Torah and teaches Torah and sends his students to visit Poland with the flag of Israel in their hands…these are such powerful feelings that one cannot indulge them so often. You have to be able to go on and study and teach.

Moshko, Rav Amital, Yediyah HaCohen, and Dr. Brayer, the ones who initiated Yeshivat Har Etzion, "knew how to instill in their students the strength of the history of Gush Etzion, the connection between the past and the future."

Approximately one hundred and fifty students attend Rav Fischer's yeshiva that stands high on a hill in Efrat. All of the students live in Efrat and absorb an intensive curriculum of Tanach, *Chassidut*, Jewish thought and Gemarah. After they complete their studies at the yeshiva, they go in a variety of directions, some to higher yeshiva studies, others to *hesder* yeshivas, some to regular army service, and some to *mechinot* – one or two year programs that prepare religious young men to sucessfully merge into regular army service. At some point, they all serve in the military.

Rav Fischer and his wife, Tziporah, live in Alon Shevut with their seven children. Tziporah works in the pedagogical library there.

Efrat was a success story, and people came to study the model before they undertook to build other *yishuvim*. At one point the government minister in charge of building new areas came to Moshko and said: "It is your luck that we didn't believe you would succeed. If we had thought you would succeed, we would not have let you try. What is this? we asked ourselves. A private individual comes with a request to build a new *yishuv*? We never heard of such a thing. "Today," Moshko says with justified pride, "*Baruch Hashem*, more than a thousand families live in Efrat – over 10,000 people. Today there is a housing shortage in Efrat."

Dan & Estanne Abraham
860 Fifth Avenue
New York 10021

November 5, 1980

Mr. and Mrs. Moshe Moskovics
Masuot Yitzhak
Doar Na, Lachish Tzafon
Israel

Dear Mr. and Mrs. Moskovics:

We are pleased to invite you to join us at a reception we are giving in
honor of Rabbi Shlomo Riskin and Mr. Moshe Moskovics.

Rabbi Riskin is known to most of us as the Rabbi of the Lincoln Square
Synagogue and the founder of Jewish high schools in the Greater New
York area. He is now deeply involved with an aliya movement and the
educational structure of the new town in Israel known as Efrat.

Mr. Moskovics is presently the Chief Advisor in the Ministry of Interior
of the State of Israel. He is the founder of Gush Etzion, developer of
the entire Shafir region, and the prime moving force in Israel in the
development of Efrat. He is a most interesting and important person.

During this reception you will have the opportunity to hear an exciting
report about Efrat and the entire Gush Etzion area. Please understand
that our guests will not be asked to make any commitments but we do
want you to learn about developments in this crucial area of Israel
which is assuming great strategic importance in these difficult and
unsettled times.

This reception will take place on Monday, November 24th, 8:00 pm, at
our home, 860 Fifth Avenue, Apt. 19B (at 68th Street). Kindly respond
on the enclosed card letting us know that you will join us that
evening.

Looking forward to greeting you on the evening of the 24th.

Sincerely,

Estanne & Dan Abraham

Invitation to meet Moshko in New York to hear about
the dream of Efrat Nov. 5, 1980

Chapter VII
Herzog College

A N EVENING in May 1995 – 10 PM: Rav Shmuel Vigoda is sitting in the living room of his home talking with his wife and
children. Exhausted from the day's long field trip to the Negev with
the Jerusalem Fellows, he had returned only an hour before. The
phone rings, and he answers. Looking on, his wife is worried as
she sees her husband face turn ashen.

Hanging up the phone after a very short conversation, Rav
Vigoda, still looking stunned, turned to his family. Many thoughts
swirled through his head. He loved his work in Jewish education
and was slated to become director of the prestigious Jerusalem
Fellows program. The Jerusalem Fellows program was created in
1981 by Seymour Fox and facilitated by Arye Dulzin. Dulzin was
a prominent Zionist leader who served for ten years as treasurer
of the Jewish Agency and World Zionist Organization, eventually
becoming head of both agencies. He also was a governor of Bank
Leumi which sponsored the Jerusalem Fellows.

"At the other end of the phone," Rav Vigoda said to his anxious
family, "was Rav Lichtenstein, who spoke in his usual short and very
concise style: 'This is Rav Lichtenstein; how are you. You know that
we have a college. The director of the college is about to take a year

off, and I would like you to take that directorship. It may become permanent, but we don't know at the present time. All that I can offer you now is one year.'"

It was May, late in the academic year, and Rav Vigoda had already promised to head up the Jerusalem Fellows. He did not make promises lightly. "But, all those years, I was always very close to Rav Lichtenstein. At every signicant crossroads in my career, I consulted with him; I saw him as "my rebbe." And now he had the confidence in me to offer me this position as head of Herzog College."

Rav Aharon Lichtenstein has extremely high standards and, when he chooses someone for a top position, excellence is an expectation, not a goal. In Shmuel Vigoda he had turned to a man of broad and deep experience in every aspect of Jewish education, especially pedagogy – ways of teaching, methodology of curriculum building, the very basic sciences of educational instruction.

Born in Strasbourg, France, in 1953, Rav Vigoda was educated in that city's Jewish institutes of education. Strasbourg has a Jewish community of approximately 15,000, with a strong religious component, both Ashkenazi and Sephardi.

Rav Vigoda's father was born in Poland and made his way to France after the war. Though his mother was born in France, her parents were also from Poland. Both parents grew up in religious families. "My father regularly invited Jewish students for Shabbat meals. One of them was an Israeli who was studying dentistry in Strasbourg. I learned from him about high school students coming to Israel to study in a yeshiva. I raised the idea of studying in Israel, but my parents were reluctant, because it was unheard of for a kid of fifteen to leave home and study abroad." Nevertheless, he convinced them to let him have his way.

Shmuel, the oldest of three boys, traveled to Israel in 1968 to study at Midreshet Noam. Finishing high school there, he went on to spend one year at Yeshivat Kerem Beyavneh, after which he transferred to Yeshivat Har Etzion. At the time there was no *hesder* program for non-Israeli students, so he went into the army after one year of study, serving in a *machal* unit. *Machal* is an acronym for *Mitnadvei Chutz L'aretz* – volunteers from outside Israel. After serving as a paratrooper, he returned to his studies at Har Etzion for three years. Following those three years, he began his studies in education and philosophy at The Hebrew University.

Married, with one child, Rav Vigoda accepted the challenge of establishing the first Zionist yeshivah high school in France. The Zionist yeshiva in Paris took up most of his time, but Rav Vigoda also taught courses at two other high schools in Paris.

Returning to Jerusalem in 1982, he completed work toward *smicha* – rabbinic ordination. He completed his exams with the late Rav Fink of Haifa, Rav Yehudah Gershuni and Rav Ovadia Yosef. Having received *smicha*, he began teaching at different schools in Israel.

In 1984 he was recommended for the Jerusalem Fellows program. Seymour Fox, the director, was a knowledgeable educational leader of Conservative Jewry in America. As a dean at the Jewish Theological Seminary, he was instrumental in starting the Ramah summer camps, including two in Israel. He had particular expertise in curriculum development, and Rav Vigoda learned a great deal from him in his three years as a Jerusalem Fellow.

In 1987, at the end of his three-year fellowship, Rav Vigoda planned to fulfill the requirement for three years of service in the Diaspora, a condition built into the Jerusalem Fellows program. After making plans to return to France for the three-year period, he was made aware of an opportunity in Canada.

"Until that day, I had never been on the North American continent. I agreed to go for an interview only because I was tempted to see what America is all about. I did not think anything serious would come of it, but I was offered the job. I accepted, because I felt that, in order to be a leader in Jewish education, not to know what was going on in the American world would have been a mistake."

Montreal is a largely French-speaking community, but Rav Vigoda became head of a school that was fully anglophile. He found some things that he expected; in other areas he was disappointed: "I found the standards and quality to be higher than those I knew in Europe. The school I directed had five hundred students, from kindergarten through high school. The level of *limudei kodesh* was incomparably higher than that of the school I had attended as a student in France. The number of hours devoted to Chumash, Gemarah, the Prophets and Jewish philosophy was infinitely greater."

So in what areas did he experience the disappoinments? Rav Vigoda had studied theories in education and curriculum development in depth with Seymour Fox at the Jerusalem Fellows, and expected these areas to have been fully developed in the United States and Canada. He vividly recalls calling Fox for help: "Look, Seymour, I am sorry to tell you, but I am probably the only school director with no organized curriculum. There are no clear objectives, no articulation of what skill levels are desired. There is no symbiosis between Jewish studies and general studies. In short, the whole array of issues that are the backbone of any serious curriculum are lacking here."

Fox asked Rav Vigoda to ascertain the situation at other leading schools in the modern Orthodox world. He contacted Ramaz and Ohr Chaim in New York, Ulpanah in Toronto, the Hebrew Academies in Washington and Miami, Maimonides in Boston and others. The lack of an organized curriculum was the norm throughout Canada and the United States.

Thus did Rav Vigoda undertake a leading role in the elaboration of a syllabus for Jewish studies in modern Orthodox day schools. A group of professionals came to Montreal for that purpose. The Mandel Institute was established by Mort Mandel of Cleveland, with Rav Vigoda's colleague from the Jerusalem Foundation, Seymour Fox serving as the academic director.

An overlapping undertaking during Rav Vigoda's years in Montreal was the convening of a unique conference on Jewish education. Mort Mandel was the driving force behind this initiative. The conference was made up of professional and lay leaders of the training institutes of Orthodox, Conservative, and Reform Jewry. There were frequent meetings over a three-year period, 1986–1989, each meeting well-organized and followed by comprehensive documentation of the reports. The final report of the three-year conference was a book called *A Time to Act*.

Mort Mandel and his brothers backed up their commitment to Jewish education by donating $750,000 each to the educational efforts of the Orthodox, Conservative, and Reform Movements.

At this point, a very important process began that helps one understand the differences, or at least perceived differences, between modern Orthodox and *charedi* Orthodox communities. Torah Umesorah, the largest Jewish Day School organization in America, largely identified with the *charedi* world turned to Mr. Mandel and asked: "How could you have left us out of your generous pledge?"

Rav Vigoda recalls his own reaction to Torah Umesorah when he arrived in Canada: "When I first came to the Hebrew Academy in Montreal in 1987, the school was affiliated with Torah Umesorah. I withdrew it from them and affiliated with Yeshiva University. The issues were clear to me; there were good guys and bad guys, and we weren't going to be affiliated with the "black hatters." Yeshiva University was the home of Rav Soloveitchik, the home of my rav, Rav Lichtenstein; I have nothing to do with the *charedi* guys."

Back in Jerusalem, after five years in Montreal, Rav Vigoda continued his important work in Jewish education as senior researcher for the Mandel Institute. It was in this role that he was asked to look into the Torah Umesorah organization, with an eye toward a decision on their request for funds. Rav Vigoda reflects on the irony of the situation:

"Here I was, an Orthodox Jew working for the Mandel Institute. Mort Mandel is a Reform Jew, and his academic director, Seymour

Fox is a Conservative Jew. And here I am, consulting back in America, sitting in the headquarters of Torah Umesorah, a *charedi* group. I was shocked at what I learned."

The leaders of Torah Umesorah told Rav Vigoda up front that they knew what they had and what they did not have. They explained that they had over 150,000 students in their system and 3,000 instructors teaching *limudei kodesh* – religious studies. "I have to say in all humilty, they said right out that they were looking for guidance. They were honest and straightforward."

The Mandel family made a $200,000 gift to Torah Umesorah as opposed to $750,000 to the Orthodox, Conservative and Reform movements. Together with Rav Vigoda, they decided to create a teacher's training program at the largest Torah Umesorah Kollel in the United States – Lakewood, New Jersey. Working closely with Rav Vigoda were Rabbis Joshua Fishman and David Bernstein. "We created a program that was limited in scope, but was light years ahead of anything that existed up to that point. The climate of confidence and of real partnership between them and us was something that I cherished very much."

It was Rav Vigoda's background of experience and depth of knowledge that Rav Aharon Lichtenstein had in mind when he turned to him to become head of Herzog College.

In 1973, Israel's Ministry of Education came to recognize the lack of male teachers for *limudei kodesh* in the state-operated religious schools. As a result, they turned to Yeshivat Har Etzion to create a teacher's training program. The idea was clear – there was a pool of talented, bright, idealistic young religious men who were learning Torah in a very serious way. If these young men could get the training to become competent teachers, they could bring a wealth of knowledge and enthusiasm to the state religious school system. Thus was the Yaacov Herzog teacher's program created.

The program was initially very limited in scope, but has grown considerably. Rav Vigoda explains: "Twenty-five years ago, what one needed to be certified as a teacher was minimal. The training program we had consisted of a few courses in psychology and a little bit of didactics. We grew as the requirements increased. A two-year training period became the norm for teacher certification, then three years, and in the early 1990s, the Ministry of Education required all teachers to have a bachelor's degree."

Meanwhile, the teacher training program within the yeshiva became the Yaacov Herzog Training Institute. Now the decision had to be made whether or not to become a college granting a bachelor's degree. It was a major commitment and, as in everything else the yeshiva did, the college had to be held to the highest standards of excellence. When a decision was made to move ahead, the request for full certification was presented and, in 1997, Herzog College was awarded complete recognition as an academic institution granting a bachelor's degree in Education.

It was no surprise when teachers already in the field came to Rav Vigoda and said: "It is a pity that we cannot benefit from these great teachers. We would like to have the opportunity to study as well, to increase our skills. Why can't you organize a *hishtalmut* – in service training."

From this request began a Sunday learning program, first for teachers from the Gush, then the entire Jerusalem area, and finally from all over the country. Rav Vigoda explains why, in Israel, in-service training is much more developed than in the United States: "First, in Israel, the more in-service training one takes, the more the salary level is raised. Secondly, many people who are certified to teach in elementary school cannot teach in middle school without a special upgrading of their certification. And third, many people want to come and learn *Torah lishma* – the study of Torah for its own sake, regardless of the other two considerations."

While the project was initially for male teachers, a separate track for women was created, first outside Efrat, then in Alon Shevut near the Yeshiva. The program grew following requests from other yeshivas for extra training for their teachers. Such is now provided for approximately one thousand students from thirty yeshivas.

At Herzog College there is a special center for the study of Tanach. Four different approaches are taught, including one dealing with biblical criticism, headed up by Rav Breuer, a recent Israel Prize winner in Torah, and a literary approach introduced to the college by Rav Yoel Bin Nun.

In practice, the four approaches are combined. The staff goes to remote areas of Israel to organize conferences on pedagogy – how to teach a particular book of the Bible or even a particular *parasha* (portion). In addition, journals and books are published on the various topics. Each summer, two days of intensive studies are held at the college, followed by tours to pertinent areas of Israel.

Rav Vigoda speaks with great pride about the development of the Women's College. The women now study in a new building of the first new campus built expressly for women's religious studies in Israel.

In 2002, Herzog College graduated its first group of Ethiopian students ordained to work as rabbis in their communities. "I can't begin to tell you how moving it was to be at the Chief Rabbinate and hear one of the graduates speak of the impact the training had on him and his group, on their families and the entire community," Rav Vigoda relates.

The major focus of Herzog College is the training of graduates of *hesder* yeshivas to be educators. *Hesder* students come to Herzog for an additional four years to earn a bachelor's degree. This can be in Education, Bible, Talmud, Jewish Philosophy, Hebrew Language, or Land of Israel studies. Application has been made to provide degrees in Computers, Hebrew Literature and Special Education.

Another growing program is the vtc – Virtual Teachers' College. Teachers all over the world will be able, via the Internet, to acquire lesson plans, articles, and other teaching materials they may need in any subject relating to Jewish education. A pilot project to five schools in North America has been sucessfully completed, and major foundations are being approached to help finance expansion of the program.

After the assassination of Prime Minister Yitzhak Rabin, Rav Vigoda wanted to develop a program to bridge the gap between the religious and secular worlds in Israel. The idea is to train teachers in the world of the *hesder* yeshivas to do outreach. He asked one of his teachers, Rav Shlomo Brin, to head up the program. Rav Brin remembers its beginnings:

> The idea began after Rabin's assassination. There was a recognition that there was a serious split, and what was necessary was a more basic approach to the problem – we thought that the secular public wants somehow to be connected to the culture of Torah and tradition. After the assassination, we saw that there were more and more secular people who were curious about Judaism. Perhaps, in part, from fear. If there is in Judaism the potential for the murder of a prime minister, then it is necessary to learn more about it in order to know how to deal with it....I think this is the reason that there was a wave of interest in groups getting together to talk about how to bridge the gap."

Rav Brin is very sensitive to the fears and reservations of the secular public he would like to reach:

> The difficulty we face is suspiciousness on the part of the established educational system. They are afraid there is a hidden agenda to make people *ba'alei tshuva*. We are clear that this is not our goal, rather simply to teach more Torah at a more serious level. They feel, with some justice, why should we let you come into our system to teach your concept when you won't let us come into your religious educational system to teach our world

concept. The situation today in the secular schools is one of a virtual vacuum. They learn almost nothing of Torah. There are exceptions. But they don't learn about the commentaries, about Gemarah, Jewish thought, philosophy.

The *hesder* students in Rav Brin's program have to understand the world concept of the secular student. What is his world like, what are his values? The students already have a teaching certificate from Herzog College and are brought together with secular students, teachers and administrators. This is a whole new world for them. How do these religious teachers deal with a situation of conflict in a culture in conflict with their own? How do they, as individuals, go into the secular world and continue to develop their own deep connection to Judaism that was nurtured within a system where everyone has the same values? In addition to being teachers, the yeshiva graduates become students in a very real sense.

Shlomo Brin's family came to Israel directly from the European Torah world. Many survivors of that world came to Israel to implant there all that is sacred to them.

Moshe Brin, Rav Brin's father, studied in the European yeshiva world. Because there were so few yeshivas, he like many of his peers, had to study away from home. "*Achalti teig*," he smiles remembering the Yiddish expression for the support system he enjoyed, eating meals with a different local family every day of the week. He recalls the early days following his aliyah to Israel: "I worked for my uncle who was head of Betucha Insurance. This was in Tel Aviv. That part of our family was not religious. I met my wife Tova in Tel Aviv. Tova lived in Herzliya. Her parents had come to Israel in 1933 from Galicia. Her mother was from the Auschwitz area, before it became a death camp."

When Betucha Insurance decided to open a branch in Jerusalem, Moshe Brin was asked to head it:

We didn't know anyone, and no one knew us. The boys studied in religious schools. The primary school was Beit Sefer Dugma, and the high school was Netiv Meir. When it came to choosing a *hesder* yeshiva, I wanted Shlomo to go to Har Etzion. I knew Rav Amital from contact with him here in Jerusalem. It never occurred to us that our children would marry one another. I wanted Shlomo to choose the best possible school, and in my mind it was Har Etzion. Avraham Avinu took his son to Mount Moriah to the *akedah* via the area on which the yeshiva stands. I learned from my father that the study of Torah is the highest value. When I came here I was torn by those who said it was a shame that some students sit and study all the time and don't serve in the army. The *hesder* yeshivot were the answer to the wrenching feeling I had.

Rav Shlomo Brin remembers the decision-making process: "Most of my friends went to join the first class of a *hesder* yeshiva on the Golan. My parents told me it isn't so important where most of your friends are, what is important is to study at the place of the highest excellence. My parents knew Rav Amital. I had heard about him, and there was much talk about the new young rabbi, Rav Lichtenstein, who came from the United States with a big reputation. Finally, I decided to go to Yeshivat Har Etzion. It turned out that some of my friends that began at the yeshiva on the Golan transferred to Yeshivat Har Etzion. We had learned as children about the history of Gush Etzion. This, along with the reputation of the *rashei yehiva*, most influenced my decision."

Moshe Brin has vivid memories of his son's rosh yeshiva, Rav Yehuda Amital:

He was so dedicated to the yeshiva, he was like a father to all the boys, and he took care of every aspect of the physical plant. He told me he would go into the *beit midrash* after midnight to turn

off the lights, so as not to waste money, and he would find Shlomo
studying. Rav Amital leads the prayers and his whole being is
immersed in them. To hear the students praying together during
the High Holy Days is an unforgettable experience. The intensity,
the strength, the dedication to Hashem.

He also recalls a very poignant Yom Kippur service a year after
the 1973 Yom Kippur War.

I remember when it was decided to bring Rav Lichtenstein as
rosh yeshiva alongside Rav Amital. My son was in his first year
in the yeshiva. In 1973, before *Neila* – the closing service of Yom
Kippur – young men went out to war and some of them never
returned. The next year, one year after the war, Rav Amital began
talking about the *korban tamid* (burnt offering) mentioned in the
amidah. He said that last year our yeshiva gave *korbanot* to the
State of Israel. They went out to war and didn't return. He began
to cry and could not continue. Slowly, he came down from the
bimah; Rav Lichtenstein arose and continued for him. He compared Rav Amital's depth of feeling with that of Rav Yehuda Lev
Diskin who fainted when he heard the news that his synagogue
had caught fire and fifteen Torahs had been destroyed.

Moshe Brin is grateful for the atmosphere at Yeshivat Har
Etzion:

The boys at the yeshiva learn Torah and Gemarah. They have
two great examples as rashei yeshiva. Rav Amital was born in
Hungary and Rav Lichtenstein came from a different culture in
Lita (Lithuania), yet see how they work together. There is so much
love and respect for one another that it rises above all else. The
students see this example, and they learn how to behave toward
one another. Rav Lichtenstein had his elderly parents there for

a time. His father was very ill and required a wheel chair. Rav Lichtenstein took care of his every need; he never had students do it for him.

Rav Brin remembers the Jerusalem in which he grew up. "Jerusalem before 1967 was another Jerusalem. I remember that our street, Chovevei Tzion, was not far from the border. We hid in the house when they fired shots toward our area. As children, we were afraid to walk in neighboring Yemin Moshe. If the school wanted to take students there, they had to have special permission." He recalls an occasion when he heard a great deal of noise outside the house where his parents live until the present time. The commotion turned out to be students singing "Happy Birthday" to his across-the-street neighbor – Professor Martin Buber.

KOLLEL AT ALON SHEVUT

It is quite a journey for a child from Casablanca to become *rosh kollel* at Alon Shevut, but Rav Shlomo Levi made the trek. His forebears on his father's side came from Spain to Morocco and, on his mother's side, from Tangiers to Moroco. There his parents met and married, then came to Israel in 1957. He is the third of three boys. His oldest brother, Yitzhak Levi, served for a number of years as head of Mafdal, the National Religious political party.

After five years in a *hesder* program, students generally continue in a *kollel* – a group of students studying together after their higher yeshiva education. There are ninety young men living at Alon Shevut and studying in the *kollel*. Many are married by then and study toward *smicha* – ordination as rabbis. This is generally a three-year tract, and the students take exams at the end of each year. These exams are given by the Chief Rabbinate of Israel. The members of one group in the kollel have already received *smicha* and are continuing Gemarah study at a very high, intensive level.

Rav Levi's experience at Yeshivat Har Etzion goes back to 1970.

He was in the second class at the new *hesder* yeshiva. The class began their studies in temporary quarters at Kfar Etzion, then moved to Alon Shevut. After his five years of *hesder*, Rav Levi thought about pursuing a degree at The Hebrew University, but he was asked by Rav Amital to continue at Alon Shevut. "Rav Amital had established an atmosphere of seriousness, of excellence. He always said that Alon Shevut was about the students and their advancement. There was here great unity and cooperation. I was very happy to be offered the opportunity to stay."

Rav Levi and his wife live in Neve Daniel and have eleven children. The two oldest boys study at Yeshivat Har Etzion in Alon Shevut.

Chapter VIII
Women's Studies

W HEN Rav Vigoda first began to think about women's studies, he felt strongly that this was an important element missing from Yeshivat Har Etzion. With the approval of the *rashei yeshiva*, he met with Esti Rosenberg, Rav Lichtenstein's daughter, who he felt had the qualifications to head the program. Rav Lichtenstein became enthusiastic about the idea. He recalls: "It was always a value at Yeshivat Har Etzion, but there was no preconceived notion that there would be a woman's college. Many of the most prominent teachers at the centers for women's studies in Israel are products of Yeshivar Har Etzion. They are involved at Matan, Nishmat, Bruria (Brovender), Midreshet Lindenbaum and other institutions of women's learning."

Rabbanit Rosenberg, the head of the women's college, speaks in rapid-fire Hebrew, full of enthusiasm and passion for education. Though she was born in New York and lived there until age six, Rabbanit Rosenberg remembers nothing of that period of her life. Her mother, Tovah, the daughter of Rav Soloveitchik, spoke to the children in English, and her father, Rav Lichtenstein, spoke Hebrew, even when the family lived in New York. She recalls that her mother was pregnant when they arrived in Israel. When her mother was admitted to the hospital, Esti had no contact with her, as they had no phone and children were not allowed to visit in the hospital. So during her mother's absence from home, Esti spoke only Hebrew, "and from that time on, I almost never speak English."

Rabbanit Rosenberg recalls that in school she was considered somewhat of a rebel. Attitudes toward dress and other customs were more lenient in her home than at Chorev, which, at the time, was one of only a few places a religious girl could study. "I remember that in tenth grade there was a remark on my report card that I must give in more to the opinions of my teachers. Many of my teachers were *charedim*, and I had to fight hard for what I believed in. For example, they demanded that I wear long sleeves, saying the rabbis required that. I told them that my father did not require long sleeves and that I went according to the ruling of my father."

Rabbanit Rosenberg's relief from the tense school atmosphere came from her participation in a branch of a religious youth movement. "It was very significant in my life. I was in the same youth group from the seventh grade until I was nineteen or twenty years old. I spent as much time with my friends as I could. When I left school, I closed the door behind me and never had a desire to continue the relationships I had there. It was completely different in my youth group.

"What was particularly important for me was my friendships with the boys. I had many more friends who were boys than girls. I had brothers, I studied with my father, and I was much more open to friendships with boys than were most girls my age. I spent every other Shabbat at Yeshivat Har Etzion with all the guys. The opportunities young women have today are completely different from when I was growing up. When I try to tell students today what it was like for me, they have a very difficult time relating to my experience."

Much of Rabbanit Rosenberg's experience in the youth movement was as a *madricha* – a leader and counselor. "In the end, I think the experience had more of an influence on us as *madrichim* than it did on those we led. As *madrichim* we sat until all hours of the night struggling with what we wanted and did not want. Was it all right for women to sing in the presence of men or not? Many of the children went to movies and the theater. Most of the participants were very open and I learned a great deal there to think about options in one's life. In my home, everything was very clear; you must study Torah and the path before you is prescribed and understood.

"My parents did not have the experience in a youth movement like I did. It is a very Israeli experience, and I value it a great deal. My brothers did not have the experience. They absorbed the message that you sit and you learn. They were much more serious than I was in those years. Yet, in many ways, I was raised like a boy. I prayed three times a day. When students ask me why I pray three times a day, I say it isn't a question of "why." From age seven, I was told this was what I should do. My mother does it, and I do it. It never occurred to me on Sukkot to eat outside the sukka. When I was in sixth grade, our youth group was having a *tiyul* – field trip. I was told that if there would be sukkot to eat in, I could go; if not, I could not go. In so many ways, I was raised as a boy, and I accepted it with joy. I loved it and did not suffer a bit."

However, there were clear differences in the raising of a girl in the Lichtenstein household from the manner of raising the boys. Only on Shabbat were the girls included in study. When the boys were in Beit Meir, in their high school years, Rav Lichtenstein would go to them on Mondays and Thursdays and study with them there; it was never suggested that he would do likewise with the girls during the week. In addition, the two brothers older than Rabbanit Rosenberg had the privilege to spend their 12th grade year in America studying with Rav Soloveitchik, their revered grandfather.

After high school and a year of *sherut leumi* – national service – Rabbanit Rosenberg began studying at the *Michlalah* – a women's college for religious studies. At that time there was nowhere else for a young woman to study. "Today there is no need to go to the *Michlalah*; there are women's seminaries and *batei midrash*. When I studied in the *Michlalah*, it was more Zionistic and more open from the standpoint of dress codes. My teachers included Rav Yedid, Rav Yoel Bin-Nun and Rav Mordechai Breuer. They are no longer there, but are teaching in other places, including at women's institutions that have been founded more recently.

At the *Michlalah*, Rabbanit Rosenberg was a changed student. "I always say that my high school teachers would have been jealous of my teachers at the *Michlalah*. In high school, I battled the teachers on everything they said to me. At the *Michlalah*, I knew what I wanted, and I had wonderful teachers. I observed the rules and did not argue with anyone. I wanted to finish in two years. The first year for me was very intensive and I passed twelve of the twenty exams required for the two years. There was no *beit midrash* like the girls can study in today, but I had the privilege to learn from Chana Beilinson, *zichrona livracha* – may her memory be for a blessing, Rav Epstein, and Rav David Fox, in addition to those I have already mentioned. I don't have a single bad word to say about my two years at the *Michlalah*."

Having received a teaching certificate at the *Michlalah*, Rabbanit Rosenberg attended The Hebrew University for two years studying literature and history. During this time, she also taught in Rav Riskin's high school, Neve Chana. Teaching a ninth grade class was frustrating to her, and she wanted a change, but did not know exactly what she was looking for. Just at the right time, she was recruited to work for Bnei Akiva. "Avraham Lipshitz had become the first director of Bnei Akiva who had not come from the religious kibbutz movement, a revolutionary change. Avraham Lipshitz is his own person and is very dynamic. He had established a very successful school in Tiberias, and his abilities were very much respected in our home. I remember when my father first mentioned that Lipshitz was taking the position at Bnei Akiva, there was an air of excitement about the news."

During a very intensive year working for Bnei Akiva, Rabbanit Rosenberg met her husband-to-be. He came from "a very warm home. His parents gave him all the love in the world, but he did not have a strong religious background growing up." In response to a question as to what her in-laws thought of their son marrying the daughter of Rav Aharon Lichtenstein, Rabbanit Rosenberg laughs and says: "They did not know who he was." The couple married during Chanuka, 1990.

Rabbanit Rosenberg never thought that she would continue learning, much less that she would teach high school and become the head of a school. When she decided to investigate what studies were available to her, she went to Matan, a religious women's learning center, and they suggested to her that she study Gemarah. "It never occurred to me that I would study Gemarah. I had studied with my father on Shabbat over the years, but never opened a Gemarah on my own." Rabbanit Rosenberg was placed in the top level Gemarah class and was delighted to find that she had more than a small residue of knowledge from the years she had studied with her father.

In the same year she was studying at Matan, Rabbanit Rosenberg heard that Nurit Fried was starting a woman's school in Efrat. The idea of being part of this excited her and, at her parents' urging, she called Nurit Fried and was invited to begin on the ground floor of the new endeavor. Rabbanit Fried had the entire administrative load on her shoulders, so turned to Rabbanit Rosenberg to prepare the first year of study for the seventeen girls who were enrolled. When the year began, there were classes on two mornings lacking teachers, so Rabbanit Rosenberg took them on. At the same time, she was studying three mornings at Matan.

The following year, Rabbanit Rosenberg left Matan to work full time at Bruria, a women's school in Efrat. She spent six years there and played a major role in developing Bruria into a highly successful study program for religious women.

The construction of the first campus in Israel built explicitly for women's religious studies opened its doors in 2003. It was designed by the same architect who drew up the plans for Yeshivat Har Etzion, and the common themes are majestic.

Both *rashei yeshiva* of Har Etzion also teach classes on the women's campus. Rav Amital gives a weekly class in the *Kuzari* – the classic twelfth-century exposition of Jewish thought by Rabbi Yehuda Halevi, and Rav Lichtenstein conducts a *shiur* in Gemarah.

Despite the difficult security situation in Israel in general, and in the Gush in particular, there has been an increase in the applications for the different study programs under Rabbanit Rosenberg's direction. She lives in Alon Shevut with her husband and six children.

In the Talpiot neighborhood of Jerusalem is an old hotel with no sign out front to give an indication to the passer-by of the vibrant learning that goes on inside. This is Midreshet Lindenbaum, part of the women's study program of Rav Riskin's educational institutions. It is a symbol of the cross-pollination of the two parts of Moshko's dream to make the Gush a center of Jewish learning whose influence would spread even beyond the Gush. At the inception of Midreshet Lindenbaum, Yeshivat Har Etzion graduates made up a large percentage of its educators.

The inspiring head of the *beit midrash* at Midreshet Lindenbaum is Rabbanit Malka Petrokovsky. She, like Rabbanit Rosenberg, her counterpart at the Herzog Women's College, exudes a contagious love of and passion for learning and teaching Gemarah. She provides for the young women who come to study an opportunity that was not available to her, one generation earlier.

Rabbanit Petrokovsky's parents were both *nitzulei shoah* – survivors of the Holocaust. Her Hungarian-born father and Romanian-born mother met in Israel, the haven they found after the horrors of World War II. Her late father was a *talmid chacham* – a Torah scholar whose family were *charedim*. In Israel, he became a contractor and made a living building houses and streets, part of the infrastructure of the young state to which he came in 1949.

Traditionally, a father who is a *talmid chacham* loves to study with his sons. A patient man, Rabbanit Petrokovsky's father was a doting parent to five daughters before his one son came along. His third daughter, Malka, was not so patient. "I was a *nudnikit* (nagger)", Rabbanit Petrokovsky relates. "From an early age, I loved to learn. He recognized this and taught me, and this is how my love of learning Torah began." A Torah education was not available in Ashdod where she was born, so she came to Jerusalem to study at Pelech in her high school years. "There I received a good basic education to build on what I had learned from *Abba*."

After graduation, Rabbanit Petrokovsky served two years in the army. She earned her bachelor's degree at Bar Ilan University and returned to Pelech as a teacher. At first, she taught Gemarah, Jewish history and philosophy, along with her duties as a home room teacher and young mother. Deciding that, if she wanted to be a serious educator, she had to focus her attention in one area, she began teaching only Gemarah, which remained her focus for eight years. At that point, Rabbanit Petrokovsky made an interesting change.

Temporarily leaving the religious world of learning, Rabbanit Petrokovsky studied toward her Master's degree in Talmud at Tel Aviv University, a bastion of secular education. "I wanted to teach Gemarah in the secular world. This was after the murder of Yitzhak Rabin. She was pained by this event and by the awareness that the secular world had so little exposure to Gemarah. However, shortly before obtaining her Master's degree, she was prevailed upon by Rav Riskin, who knew her talent and passion for Gemarah, to come to the *beit midrash* at Midreshet Lindenbaum. For one year, she was a *ramit* (teacher of Gemarah) and then became the head of the *beit midrash*, adding this responsibility to her first love, teaching and studying Gemarah.

Rabbanit Petrokovsky lives in Tekoa, a settlement south of Efrat. She and her husband, a graduate of a *hesder* yeshiva, have five children, two boys, and three girls. Her husband works in the high tech industry. What keeps a dedicated mother of five children working day after day as the head of a *beit midrash* for women?

"I very much respect and admire Rav Riskin. I identify completely with his concept of Jewish education – to learn Torah in depth in the most serious possible manner, to keep the mitzvot without games and posing, which is to say to make this the center of one's life. Yet, along with this to know and understand the world outside the *beit midrash*. I want our students to know all of Eretz Yisrael and all of its people, to be exposed to and understand the general community, not just the one in which they live. It is very important to be part of the entire community, not to sit in the *beit midrash* and have nothing to do with the rest of the world. We must be people of Torah, within a life in the world."

This view of the world continues that of Rabbanit Petrokovsky's father. Though coming from a *charedi* family, he insisted on enlisting in the army when he came to Israel in 1949. Very well versed in *limudei kodesh*, he might have spent his life after the Holocaust in study, but he became a contractor, a builder of Eretz Yisrael. In Israel he met and married Rabbanit Petrokovsky's mother who had also made aliyah in 1949.

Young women from the religious Zionist community stream to Midreshet Lindenbaum to deepen their understanding of *limudei kodesh*, which is to say, to deepen their connection to Hashem. They come from kibbutzim, moshavim, and cities from all over. They come from Ashkenazi and Sephardi backgrounds. There are three different learning tracts: One tract is for girls who have finished high school, one for girls who have completed their national service – an alternative to serving in the army – and an advanced program for those desiring to continue studying.

For the high school graduates, there are three possibilities. Some follow a program similar to the *hesder* program for boys. They study one year, then enter military service through an agreement between Midreshet Lindenbaum and the army. Rabbanit Petrokovsky explains: "We coordinate the program with the army. Some of the girls serve in the education corps. Others will serve in military intelligence. When they enter the army, we visit them where they are serving. They come back here often on Shabbat and occasionally for an entire day of study. The army is in contact with us about their progress."

Some high school graduates come to Midreshet Lindenbaum for a year of intensive study, after which they go on their own to the army or national service without a continuing connection to Midreshet Lindenbaum. The program of national service is of two years' duration.

The second major program is for young women who come to Midreshet Lindenbaum only after they have served in the army or done national service. They enter into a year of very intensive study "from morning till night." They learn in all areas of *limudei kodesh* – Torah, Mishnah, religious philosophy, and *chasidism*, and for sure Gemarah. Even those who have no background in Gemarah are given guidance in entering into that world.

The third program is for advanced students, those with a background in Gemarah studies. It attracts some who have completed their *hesder*-type program or their national service. The project is very structured in that there is a definite, prescribed program of study and each group is taught and supervised by a single *ram* – teacher of Gemarah. In Elul, the month prior to the High Holy Days, there are studies in the tractate of the Gemarah called "*rosh Hashanah*." In the winter, the students delve into another tractate and, after a Pesach break, continue with the same *masechet* – tractate.

In addition to these various programs for Israelis, there are approximately one hundred young women annually who come from outside Israel to study at Midreshet Lindenbaum. They are high school graduates with a background in religious studies. At Midreshet Lindenbaum, they continue those studies, and in addition are exposed to Eretz Yisrael through field trips and classes. At the end of the year, they return to their home countries, but many ultimately settle in Israel.

Chapter IX
Behind the Scenes

For every institution, there are those behind the scenes who labor consistently and tirelessly, making few demands yet making things work. For Yeshivat Har Etzion, one such person is Dr. Meyer Brayer.

Meyer Brayer was born in Rumania 1925, the son of a small-town rabbi. He was educated there in a yeshiva until, when he was fourteen, the family was chased away by the Rumanians.

Fortunate not to be deported, the family was evacuated to a larger town where the Germans and the Romanians used Jews as workers. His father was a hostage to be killed if they didn't show up for work. Meyer was active in the religious youth movement, Bnei Akiva.

After World War II, the British were barring entry to Eretz Yisrael and, as a result, many Jews sailed "illegally." Brayer was among a group of approx 350 young men from various youth organizations who, with the help of the Haganah, boarded a ship called the *Max Nordau*. The trip from Constanta, a Black Sea port in southeast Rumania, took fifteen days. As feared, they were intercepted by the British and taken to Atlit, an Israeli coastal village where the British had set up a prison.

The prison held Brayer only two days before he escaped with a small group and made his way to a kibbutz called Be'erot Yitzhak. Be'erot Yitzhak, affiliated with the religious kibbutz movement, was the first settlement in the Negev. Dr. Brayer recalls the Egyptian attack on the day Israel declared its independence, May 14, 1948:

> We were about two miles from Gaza. Anticipating an attack by the Egyptians, we began to dig trenches three months in advance. We had four underground shelters with twenty-four beds in each. There were fifty-eight married men in the kibbutz and sixty children. On Saturday morning, we lost our first member. Women and children were evacuated from the kibbutz. We lived underground almost two months, taking artillery fire every day.

The artillery attacks were meant to soften the resistance of the kibbutz prior to an Egyptian ground attack:

> In the middle of the summer, the ground attack came. Everything above ground was leveled. All we had were old Italian rifles, one crude mortar, one automatic weapon and some makeshift grenades. The Egyptians thought everyone was dead. When they came under fire from our one Beza machine gun from Czechoslovakia, they were frightened and retreated. Later we found out that Gamal Abdul Nasser was in charge of the attack. They wanted to control the Gaza-Beersheva road, but didn't succeed.

That night, Moshe Dayan came to the kibbutz and brought reinforcements. Levi Eshkol, in charge of settlement and later a prime minister of Israel, decided to move the kibbutz to the center of the country, near Petach Tikva, where it continues to flourish.

Meyer Brayer remained at Be'erot Yitzhak until 1955, when his two-year-old daughter was one of many children stuck by polio. He took his daughter to New York where his parents had settled in

1948 after leaving Rumania. The child was treated in New York for nine years and is today living a productive life in Jerusalem.

While in the United States, Dr. Brayer earned a Masters' degree and a doctorate from Yeshiva University in Biblical Literature. He served as principal of the Hebrew Institute of Long Island in Far Rockaway (today the Hebrew Academy of the Five Towns).

Back in Israel, Dr. Brayer was approached in 1969 by survivors of the Gush who wanted to establish a yeshiva. "Moshe Moskovic approached me, and I also knew Rav Amital, whose wedding had taken place at my kibbutz and who came almost every second week to teach Kuzari. So, in September 1969, I became part of the management of the yeshiva. It wasn't so easy at the beginning. I went to the United States to acquaint people with what and who we were and to raise money. Later, it was clear one person alone couldn't do that, so we hired someone in the States to spread the message and raise money."

Dr. Brayer recalls the opposition of many in the religious community to the establishment of *hesder* yeshivas, feeling that the time spent in the army took away from Torah study. "We didn't agree with that. We believe in joining the army as a duty in good and bad times, not just in time of emergencies."

Dr. Brayer is appropriately proud of how Har Etzion students have branched out to teach all over Israel and throughout the world. "One of our graduates is heading up outreach in Peru, another in Oslo, and many are working in other places. They go and stay two to three years at least. Then we try to find someone to take over for them. The Zionist Kollel has people in Cleveland, Memphis, New York, South Africa, France, Russia and many other places. A large percentage of the staff of Midreshet Lindenbaum, Rav Riskin's seminary for women's studies, are our graduates. The first class was very special. From this first class we have two *rashei yeshiva* of *hesder* yeshivas, Re'im HaCohen and Eliahu Blumensveig. Rav Yaacov Meidan is also from the first class. He is still part of our

Meyer Brayer and Yedaya HaCohen
reviewing a draft document

faculty. Rav Amital was the only teacher at that time. The first year
was at Kfar Etzion, then we moved to Alon Shevut. Three women
did their national service working in our kitchen and later married
three of our graduates."

Rav Amital's invitation to Rav Lichtenstein to come on board
as a rosh yeshiva is etched clearly in Dr. Brayer's memory. "Rav
Lichtenstein was impressed with the first class, their intelligence,
their dedication. I remember the meeting when he was asked to
come and join us. It was the beginnng of a wonderful relationship
with Rav Amital and a great day for the yeshiva. Today he is a *posek
halachah* – interpreter of Jewish law – who is consulted by people
all over the world."

Along with Meyer Brayer, Yedaya HaCohen has been involved with

Yeshivat Har Etzion from the beginning. He was born in Jerusalem to parents of Hungarian and Czechoslovakian extraction and has been part of a remarkable growth, in little more than a generation, of yeshiva education in the religious Zionist community.

HaCohen's father was raised in the Hungarian city of Munkacs, nestled in the Carpathian mountains. His parents sent him to Pressburg to study in the yeshiva of the grandson of the *Chatam Sofer*. There he met his wife, and together they moved to Israel in 1929, despite the Arab uprisings in which many Jews throughout *Eretz Yisrael* were killed. HaCohen attended Mizrachi schools, schools that, after the establishment of Israel, became known as *mamlachti dati* – national religious schools. After his primary school years, he studied at Kfar HaRo'eh, a Bnei Akiva Yeshiva.

HaCohen was working in the pioneer youth department of the Jewish Agency when he heard about the new *hesder* yeshiva to be established in Alon Shevut. He approached Rav Amital and offered his help. Thus, in addition to his job in the Jewish Agency, he took on major administrative responsibilities in the first year of Yeshivat Har Etzion's existence. He continued shouldering both tasks until 1992. From that time, he has been able to concentrate all of his considerable energies in Alon Shevut.

The HaCohen family is a model of a strong religious Zionist family. The first six children were boys, who were followed by two girls. The oldest son is a high ranking officer in the Israeli army. Two sons are *rashei yeshiva*, one being the head of the *hesder* yeshiva in Otniel. Two other sons teach Gemarah at yeshivas. Both of HaCohen's daughters are in Jewish education, teaching in Jerusalem. His children have blessed him with many grandchildren.

HaCohen has sharp memories of the rise of the religious Zionist community from a sense of inferiority, when he was a teenager, to the vibrant, confident community of today. In the northern part of Israel where he was studying, the feeling was that the non-religious community was building the country, and "we were standing on the sidelines." The earliest settlers were religious, but the land went to the socialist camp, and there were many exciting new pioneer communities springing up all over Eretz Yisrael.

As a teenager, HaCohen was once hitchhiking from Kfar HaRo'eh to Jerusalem. He was given a ride by a minister in the government, Ben Aharon, a member of the far left-wing Mapam party. "All the way in the car, he harangued me about being religious. I'll never forget; he said 'this is the last generation of religious Jews.' He is alive and well today, at age 96 anti-religious as ever."

In the midst of this anti-religious atmosphere, Rav Moshe Tzvi Neriya, a disciple of Chief Rabbi Kook and head of the Kfar HaRo'eh yeshiva, gave HaCohen and his students a strong sense of who they were and what they could become. On the day of the establishment of the State of Israel, HaCohen saw his rosh yeshiva crying. "What happened?" the students wanted to know. "Kfar Etzion has fallen to the Arabs, all the Gush has fallen." More than a hundred Jews had been killed, and Rav Neriya knew every one of them. "He gathered us together and told us that, through blood and tears, the redemption would come, and we would live to see it."

After the establishment of the State of Israel, there was a steady rise in the number of yeshivas. From a small handful, the number of yeshivas rose steadily and the pride of the religious population rose proportionally. "A pyramid must be built from its base," HaCohen explains. "I would estimate, that when I was in yeshiva at Kfar Ha-Roeh, there were no more than a thousand students in yeshivas throughout Israel. A solid grade school religious system had to be built, then junior high classes, then the high school yeshivas." This was done systematically, and the *hesder* yeshivas were built on the solid foundation of these programs.

Behind the scenes for Rav Riskin are two remarkable women. Above the Supersol on Agron Street is an apartment building, not very attractive from the outside. Inside however, in Apartment

33, is a charming apartment with an even more charming *ba'alat habayit* – woman of the house. The transition from Lincoln Center to Efrat would not have happened without Nina Freedman. In 1979 she was the person handling registration of people in New York interested in the move to Efrat. For the details of the move she was in ongoing contact with Moshko and his staff. "A most wonderful and serious woman!" Moshko smiles at the mention of her name and the memories of their cooperation.

Nina traces her family roots to Russia and Antwerp. She chants a beautiful *nigun* – tune – for *Menucha V'simcha* that has been passed down for many generations by her father's side of the family. Her father, Simon Schiff, came to London from Tarnów in 1890. Through two sisters who lived in Antwerp, he met Flore Moed and they were married in 1921. Nina, their third child, was born in London in 1934. Nina met her husband, Paul Cohen, in Israel in the late 1950s, and after working in Israel a few years, they moved to America, Paul's country of origin. There Nina gave birth to Khashi, Binyamin and Gideon. In New York she met Rabbi Riskin, and as she paved the way for many members of Lincoln Square to move to Israel, so too did she prepare for her own family's return.

Khashi was the first to move to Israel. He attended Sha'alvim, a *hesder* yeshiva and served in the army in the early 1980s. His brother, Binyamin, was not far behind. Both boys received *smicha*. Gideon, Nina's youngest son, also attended yeshiva at Sha'alvim, but decided there were enough rabbis in the family, so stopped short of getting *smicha*.

Nina and Paul led many trips to Israel before finally moving in 1991. Paul, ordained as a rabbi at the Jewish Theological Seminary, for many years headed up the United Synagogue Youth and introduced many American young people to Israel through seminars and tours.

Nina Cohen counts herself as among the most fortunate of people. She lives in Israel surrounded by her family. Her sister

Mickey Mirvis – Rav Riskin's indispensible "right hand"

Hélène resides in Raanana and her brother Charles in Jerusalem. Thus all of the descendants of Simon and Flore Schiff live in Israel, after only a one generation sojourn in America and England.

"You better buy quickly," Moshko said. "Over here will be the Beit Knesset, and over there will be the first school." It was 1981, and Mickey and Yonatan Mirvis could only shake their heads as they followed Moshko's moving finger. Moshko saw synagogues and schools, and they saw barren hills with rocks, rocks and more rocks. Trusting that "if Moshko says it will be good, it will be good," Mickey and Yonatan bought a future home site in Efrat in 1983.

Just as Moshko had sold his vision of Efrat to Rav Shlomo Riskin, he sold it to Mickey who was to become Rav Riskin's "right hand" in all of his many and diverse endeavors. The story of South African aliyah is an inspiring one of dedication and adventure. It was an adventure with a very happy ending. There are no more delighted Israelis than the former Bnei Akiva youth of South Africa who dreamed together of living in Israel and made the dream come true.

A high percentage of South African Jews are descendants of Lithuanian immigrants, and Mickey and Yonatan are part of that pattern. Yonatan's grandparents on both sides were Lithuanians, as were Mickey's grandpaents on her mother's side. While South African Jews have done very well, socially and economically, in South Africa, Yonatan explains the reality: "There was not what you call a South African identity. The dominant political identity was that of the Boers, and it was a religious identity. Therefore the Jews found themselves in a situation where they were not a part of the blacks, and they definitely were not part of the Boers. The whites were basically British anti-Semites. The Jewish community always knew that their sojourn was a temporary one. Of all the friends of my youth only one remains in South Africa today."

It is interesting that most South African Jews did not grow up *frum*. "I am one of the only people in my generation who has first cousins born into a *frum* family," Yonatan explains. Jewish homes were traditional but not *shomer shabbat* – Sabbath observant. Many young people became frum through Bnei Akiva, a religious Zionist youth movement.

Yonatan came to Israel in 1973, while Mickey was born in Israel. She recalls their early romance which began when she was twelve years old: "I was twelve and he was fifteen. His class came to Israel on a trip. On Yom Kippur, we were in shul and Rabbi Rabinowitz said to my father that he and his wife were invited out for the break-the-fast; could we have this young man over who was with him? So Yonatan came over and we met. He went home and told his friend he met the woman he was going to marry. When he came back to Israel, he looked me up."

Going to Israel to study in a *hesder* yeshiva was very unusual then for South Africans. Yaacov Katz, the younger brother of Yonatan's mother, was the first to take the step, in 1961. He married Moshko's daughter, Shulamit, bringing Yonatan into Moshko's extended family. Yonatan's older brother, Howard, came to the same *hesder* yeshiva, Kerem Beyavneh, and Yonatan soon followed. A younger brother, Efraim, was the first of the family to study at Yeshivat Har Etzion. He is now a rabbi in London.

Both Mickey and Yonatan knew of Rabbi Riskin before he came to Efrat, so their enthusiasm, fired by Moshko, only grew when they heard of his impending move to Efrat. Mickey knew of him when she lived in New York, where her father represented Israel at the consulate there; the first home in which Rabbi Riskin gave a talk in South Africa was the home of Yonatan's parents.

"We moved to Efrat in 1985," and it was for Mickey "like coming to Gan Eden. We had three children and they could run around freely, and it was physically a beautiful, well-planned place. You knew which family you were in seniority by the number assigned to you at the supermarket," Yonatan adds. "We were family number one-hundred and fifty-eight."

Moshko keeps coming back to Yonatan's mind at every stage of his memories of Efrat. "He deserves such enormous credit, yet he is the most modest of men. His home today would fit into a living room in Efrat. He is a man who thinks big – he can talk the language of people who are going to build these mansions, but he has kept his own personal lifestyle within the modesty of a true pioneer. Efrat has a dual mentality of a yishuv and of a city. Your home is your home, and there is great respect for privacy. Yet it has the feel of a city."

Mickey's mother tried to discourage her from moving to Efrat. "She said I should go to Ramot where my sister lives. In Efrat, she feared everyone would look into each other's yard and there would be no privacy. It's not like that. You have your privacy, but there is also a tremendous feeling of community."

Being the right hand of Rav Riskin, a man of prodigious drive and energy, is a challenging, fascinating and enjoyable job for Mickey, whose degree is in Occupational Therapy. She finished her degree just before her family left for *shlichut* (emissary work) to South Africa. When she returned, she had two children and was offered the job of working for Rav Riskin. She thought of it as a temporary job "until we get the kids settled and we all get the knack of things living in Efrat." Now she has four children, definitely has the knack of things in Efrat, but no longer thinks of her demanding job as temporary. Besides teaching, building institutions and fund raising, Rav Riskin does a great deal of individual and family counseling and is called on frequently for halachic decisions and mediation between Jews and Jews and between Jews and Arabs. The central address for coordinating all of these activites is Mickey Mirvis.

All this is not to mention typing Rav Riskin's weekly Torah portion column which appears in the press in Israel and in the United States. This is frequently done at 10:30 at night, with Yonatan being the proofreader.

Yonatan, besides having *smicha*, has an M.S. in Jewish studies and a Ph.D. in adult education. He is engaged in very rewarding work at the Melton Center of The Hebrew University where he teaches. He is also the international director of the Florence Melton Mini-School Institute.

"Florence Melton had this vision twenty-five years ago that American Jewry was deprived of Jewish education, and that the future of the community depended on the adults rather than the kids. She felt the adults were ignorant of Jewish issues, embarrassed to say so, and feeling estranged from their roots." She wanted to build a program that would not be intimidating or intrusive, one that would not call on estranged Jews to become *baalei tshuvah*. She wanted to establish a systematic structure with well-defined building blocks. She called it a mini-school because it was a part-time educational venture.

The project began in 1980 and is now in sixty cities worldwide, including the United States, Canada, England, and Australia. Twenty thousand adults are graduates of the program; currently there are over five thousand studying every week.

While separated from Jerusalem by a beautiful twenty minute drive, Efrat and the other settlements of Gush Etzion are very much involved in Israeli's body politic. In the Barak government, four ministers were residents of the Gush. The youth of Efrat is greatly "over-represented" in the Israeli armed forces. When Shlomo, Mickey and Yonatan's oldest, graduated officer's candidate school, he was one of four from Efrat. The other three Mirvis children are Tamara, Dana and Elana.

Chapter X
Passing Through the Diaspora

Many American Jews have come to Israel to be involved in serious Torah studies. Their European roots generally go back only two or three generations. Thus, in the longer perspective of history, it is clear that America was only a short sojourn for these families.

A good illustration of the common bond between Yeshivat Har Etzion in Alon Shevut and Efrat is the Koppel family. Moshe Koppel, a professor of mathematics at Bar Ilan University, studied at Yeshivat Har Etzion in the 1970s, between his sophomore and junior years at Yeshiva University (YU). He received *smicha* from YU as well as a Ph.D. in Mathematics from New York University in 1979, following which he worked at the Institute for Advanced Studies at Princeton.

Moshe's parents were both born in Eastern Europe, thus the passage through America was brief. His father, Yerachmiel Koppel, comes from a long line of Gerer Chassidim in Poland, and his mother, Gitta, also boasts a chassidic lineage from Poland and Hungary. Their oldest son, Moshe's older brother, David, also lives in Efrat. He and his wife have four children. Moshe's younger sister, Bracha, lives with her husband and four children in Beit Shemesh.

Moshe's wife, Channah Shmidman Koppel, is one of the four children of Rabbi Josh and Sabrina Shmidman of New York. Their family tree goes back to Lithuania, where Channah's paternal grandfather was a Rabbi, and to Rumania. Carrying on the rabbinical line is Channah's brother, Abie Shmidman, a Yeshiva University graduate currently serving as a rabbi in Birmingham, Alabama.

Moshe Koppel's research at Bar Ilan University is concentrated in the area of artificial intelligence. He is author of two works, *Meta Halacha,* published in English, and a book in Hebrew: *Seder Kinnim: A Mathematical Commentary on Tractate Kinnim.* He is also a founding member of The Israel Policy Center, an institute made up of leading Israeli lawyers, academics and journalists who are dedicated to breaking the stranglehold on Israeli policy and legislation held by "a small, unelected, and largely self-appointing elite, chiefly based in the judiciary and the civil service."

Moshe and Channah's very successful *aliyah* is crowned by four children, Shmuel, Shlomo, Rachel and Malka.

Dr. Meyer Brayer, one of Yeshivat Har Etzion's top administrators, is grateful for the process of "passing through America," for it is to this process that he owes his good fortune of being assisted for many years by Debbie Friedman. Debbie was born in Pittsburgh, the youngest of four children from a religious family. Her parents, both survivors of the Holocaust, and grandparents are of Polish background. Debbie was educated at the Hillel Academy of Pittsburgh, then finished high school in a Beit Yaacov school in Cleveland. She received a degree in Biology from Stern College, worked briefly on Wall Street, then married and moved to Israel in 1984. Her parents moved to Israel the same year.

Debbie's husband, Mordechai Friedman, teaches Gemarah in

the overseas program at Yeshivat Har Etzion. He was raised in Long Beach, California, where his father was head of the Hebrew Academy. After graduating Yeshiva University with a degree in computer science, he worked one year for IBM, then came to Israel and studied in the Har Etzion Kollel for three years. Debbie and Mordechai have seven children, all born in Israel.

Debbie Friedman –
administrative assistant

The value of *pru u'revu* – be fruitful and multiply – is seen over and over in religious families, a pattern which guarantees Jewish continuity. Debbie's older brother is the only one of her three siblings who is not religious. He lives in the United States and has only one child. Her second oldest brother is a businessman in Far Rockaway, New York, is religious and has five children. Her sister lives in London and has a family of seven. It is not difficult to predict that many of Debbie's nieces and nephews will, at some point, make aliyah.

Debbie loves her life in Alon Shevut. "There is a great degree of warmth and dedication to the overseas students. This is a very important year in their lives and they are privileged to learn from two *rashei yeshiva* who are *gedolei hador* – giants of the generation."

Commuting from Alon Shevut to his job as a senior financial advisor at Bank Mizrachi on Ben Yehudah Street in Jerusalem is Ari Jacobs. He and his wife Esther and their five children also value their quality of life in Alon Shevut. This is another family tree, most of whose members left Poland and Russia, passed through America for one generation, then made aliyah. Though Ari's grandparents are not alive, they leave behind fourteen great-grandchildren, eleven of whom live in Israel. Ari's younger brother is still in Baltimore, but his family came to Israel in 1995, and his sister's family came in 1996. She and her husband live in the Har Nof section of Jerusalem with their six children.

Ari's entire family is religious. "I think I'm the only one who is not *charedi*," he laughs. After high school at Chaim Berlin in New York, he studied at Yeshiva University where he earned a bachelor's degree and received *smicha*. After acquiring an MBA at Baruch College, he worked in banking for eleven years in New York. Ari met his wife, Esther, at a weekend retreat, and they were married in 1983. Her grandparents were born in Europe, but came to America where her father and mother were born. She is the only one of three children who made aliyah. One brother lives in New York with his wife and seven children and another brother is a rabbi in San Diego. Like Ari, Esther was educated in New York Jewish schools. Before moving to Israel, she worked as a programmer.

Their first four children, Malka, Yehuda, Shmuel and Shoshanna were born in the States. In 2000, Tzvi was born in Israel.

Ari and Esther always thought about aliyah, but a trip to Israel for Pesach in 1991 with Ari's parents and siblings strongly fanned the flames. In 1994, they made a pilot trip, during which Ari found that his prospects for a job in banking were good. The following year, the family moved into the absorption center in Mevaseret Tzion. At the end of a successful year of absorption, they moved to Har Nof. From a neighbor who was a student at Yeshivat Har Etzion, they learned about a new neighborhood rising in Alon Shevut and began building.

They love the atmosphere in the small *yishuv* of Alon Shevut. Their children attend school there and are well settled as Israelis.

Two other clans who passed through America and joined the *kippa s'ruga* community in Israel are the Roth and Moss families. The

Roths are an example of parents who were led to aliyah by one of their children.

The European roots of Larry and Marsha Roth go back only a few generations. Larry's father was first generation American. He was one of four children whose father came to America from Lithuania and whose mother arrived on American shores from Rumania. Both came from Orthodox Jewish homes. Larry's mother was also first generation American, her family having come from Lithuania. They were traditional Jews but did not consider themselves Orthodox.

Marsha's father came to America from Rumania in 1920; her mother, born in Massachusetts, was the daughter of parents born in Russia. When Larry and Marsha were married in 1967, they considered themselves Conservative Jews.

In 1967, the Roths were part of a large non-Orthodox Jewish population in the United States that was rapidly assimilating. Had they remained in the United States, the future of their children and grandchildren likely would have been very different from what it is today. They enrolled their children in Jewish Day Schools and, in 1979, brought David and Daniel, then ten and four years old, to Jerusalem for a year. David was not enrolled in a religious school, but, after several months, began wearing a *kippa*. In the summer of 1980, he announced to the family that he was going to make aliyah when he was eighteen.

Back in the United States after an exciting year in Israel, the Roths changed their affiliation from Conservative to Orthodox and became more and more observant. Though David attended a private, secular high school, he continued to wear a kippa at all times. When he said to his mother that he wanted to study at a *hesder* yeshiva, Marsha burst out: "What is that?" David explained and reminded her that she had raised him to be a Zionist. "He shamed me into it," Marsha says smiling.

Good to his pledge many years earlier, five days before his

eighteenth birthday, David made aliyah. Like that of many trailblaz-
ers, his experience was not easy. At Birkat Moshe, a *hesder* yeshiva
in Maaleh Adumim, he found classmates of the highest caliber
whose Hebrew was far superior to his own. When it came to his
army service, his asthma kept him from serving in a combat unit.
He volunteered to work in the Gaza Strip in civil administration
and received an award as an outstanding soldier from then General
Matan Vilnai, who subsequently became a government minister.

David finished his studies, spending some time in Rabbi
Riskin's Ohr Torah Yeshiva in Efrat, and completed his *hesder* program at the yeshiva in Sha'alvim.

After *hesder,* David studied at Bar Ilan University, where he met
his wife, Talya. Talya, who was born in the United States, comes
from a family of religious Zionists. Her great-great grandfather on
her mother's side was Yehoshua Stampfer, one of three founders
of Petach Tikva, whose son, Tania's great-grandfather, was the first
mayor of the city.

Talya's older brother came to Israel alone at age thirteen. He
was in one of Rabbi Riskin's first classes. He is now married, with
three children. Talya's father is Professor Monty Penkower, a noted
Jewish historian. She has a Master's in Psychology from Bar Ilan
University. She and David have three children, Nachson, born in
1995, Elisha, born in 1998, and Orli, born in 2003.

David's pioneering efforts smoothed the way for his brother
Daniel. Daniel, who says he "did not know the word Torah" in his
early life, studied at the Jerusalem Hartman Institute in his high
school years. He found this very suitable for an *oleh* – immigrant.
Because he desired to study Talmud in greater depth, he went into
a *mechina* (preparatory) program at Yeshivat Har Etzion, then integrated into the regular *hesder* program.

Daniel's studies at the yeshiva in Alon Shevut were challenging
and rewarding. The Brisk method of Gemarah study "is a beautiful structure. Gemarah exists regardless of history." Even though

he sees the number of students willing to take on this difficult structure diminishing, he knows the Brisk method is a fixture at Yeshivat Har Etzion. Daniel's wife, Leora, is from a strong Israeli modern-Orthodox family. Leora and Daniel live in Jerusalem. They have one child named Uriel.

The Moss family has much in common with the Roths. In the family tree of David and Rosalyn Moss, one searches back only two generations to find European roots. David's grandparents on both parents' side came from Russia, except for his mother's mother, who was fourth generation American. And, like Marsha and Larry Roth, Rosalyn and David Moss passed through America.

Rosalyn and David met as students in Israel. Roz was on her junior year abroad, studying at The Hebrew University, and David was spending a year in Israel after graduating St. John's College in New Mexico. He too was taking courses at The Hebrew University. A year later "we ran into each other again at Camp Ramah in Wisconsin."

David was born into a Reform Jewish family in Ohio, while Roz came from a *frum* family and attended a Torah Umesorah Day School in Chicago.

Married in 1971, they were drawn to Berkeley, California, where David was artist in residence at the Judah Magnes Museum. David Moss, producer of the Moss *Hagaddah*, one of the best-known Judaica artists in the world, showed no artistic bent in childhood; he became interested in Judaica only in college. "It came as a surprise to me; it came late and slowly." Although he had received an excellent education in Western civilization, he felt he knew little about Jewish culture. Thus he came to Israel where, serendipitously, he met Roz.

Berkeley, Roz explains, was "a real coming of age place for us. We started a family there and really loved it, but Jewishly it wasn't where we wanted to raise our children. Israel was always in our minds. We didn't explicitly think of aliyah, but it was always there somewhere."

With children aged four years, three years and four months, the Moss family came to Israel in 1980 for a sabbatical year. In order to finance the year, David searched for a project. A man who collected *Haggadas* knew of David's work with *ketubas* (marriage contracts) and commissioned him to do a *Haggada*. Thus was born the project that led to the famous Moss *Haggada*. After a rewarding experience in Israel, the Moss familiy returned to Berkeley where they planned their aliyah two years later.

Jackie, the youngest of the Moss children, was born in 1985, after the family moved to Israel.

It is 11 AM, *erev Yom Kippur*, and a remarkable gathering is taking place high in an apartment building on Jabotinsky Street in Jerusalem. Efrat residents David and Michael Kupietsky join their brother Ari, a Jerusalemite, at the home of their parents, Nachman and Elke Kupietsky. The joyous sounds of the proud couples' seventeen grandchildren fills the large living/dining room, attesting to an enormously successful aliyah that took place in 1973.

This branch of the Kupietsky family passed through America for only one generation. Nachman's father, Rabbi Jacob Kupietsky, was born in Lomza, Poland. He studied with the legendary Chafetz Chaim in Europe, then came to Israel where he studied with, and received *smicha* from, Israel's first chief rabbi, Avraham Yitzhak HaCohen Kook. From there, he traveled to South Africa before settling in New York. He and his wife, Fanny Dressner Chernowitz, raised four children. Nachman, their second child is the only one of the four to move to Israel. His older brother, Rabbi Jonah Kupietsky, is a congregational rabbi in Manhattan, younger brother Moshe practices law in Los Angeles, and younger sister Channah lives on Long Island.

Nachman's father was the rabbi of B'nai Jacob, a Young Israel synagogue in New York. His mother, Fanny, became involved in catering events at the synagogue, and that was the beginning of

Kay Catering which grew to be a large, successful business that now reaches down to the third generation of Kupietskys. Kay Catering became the official caterer of Rav Riskin's Lincoln Square Synagogue many years ago and continues to provide that service to this day.

Nachman recalls vividly being the captain of the debating team of Brooklyn Talmudic Academy when he was in high school. The first year, the debating team was "so-so," but the next year a student "a grade lower than me came to the Academy. He was brilliant. He was immediately put in the highest level *shiur* at the Academy and what a debater!" The student's name was Shlomo Riskin, then known as Steven.

Nachman was awarded a bachelor's degree at Yeshiva University in Religious Education, and attended the Teacher's Institute there. After Elke and Nachman became the parents of three boys, they became concerned about their safety in the streets of New York and embarked on aliyah in 1973. After initially working for a London hotelier, Nachman started his own catering business, managing events first in Savyon, where they lived the first seven years, and later in Jerusalem where they have lived for over twenty years.

Nachman and Elke's three boys have made them justifiably very proud. The two oldest boys, Ari and David, studied first at the Dov Revel Yeshiva in the United States, then at Netiv Meir in Jerusalem. Ari went on to receive *smicha* and a dental degree. He and his wife, Allison Gedalia Kupietsky, live in the Sha'arei Chesed neighborhood of Jerusalem with their seven children. David received a degree in Architecture from the Haifa Technion and lives in Efrat with his wife, Janet, and their four children.

The third son, Michael, has become a noted artist of fine Judaica. He was the originator of the kiddush cup, from which wine flows down through spouts to fill a number of smaller cups. He has been commissioned to do pieces in Israel and in the United States. Along with brother David, he lives in Efrat. He and Daphne Eisenberg Kupietsky have six children.

FROM LITHUANIA THROUGH SOUTH AFRICA TO ERETZ YISRAEL

Lithuania holds an honored place in the continuity of the Jewish people. A Jewish presence is recorded in Lithuania as early as the mid-fifteenth century. At the end of that century, the Jews were expelled, only to be courted to return in the first decade of the sixteenth century.

Poland and Lithuania were wedded in a commonwealth from 1569 until 1712, though the Jews of Lithuania fared better than their Polish brethren. They gave refuge to many Polish Jews fleeing from persecution by the Cossacks in the mid-seventeenth century. When the Russian hordes also swept into Lithuania, life became bitter for the Jews, who were confronted with endless restrictive legislation and pogroms. It is clear that the more the Lithuanian leadership was tied to the Catholic Church, the worse the situation became for the Jews.

Coming into the modern era, Lithuanian Jewry was an amalgam of immigrants from Palestine, Turkey, Syria, Iraq, Germany and Europe. "The end product," writes Masha Greenbaum in her well-researched book, *The Jews of Lithuania* (Gefen Publishing House, 1995), "was the Litvak, the Lithuanian Jew, member of a community with its own perspective of the surrounding Jewish world."

The long era of brilliant Jewish scholars began with Elijah ben Solomon Zalman – the Vilna Gaon – also known as "the Gra." Like most of the Talmud scholars who would follow him, the Gra was also knowledgable about secular matters. He stressed the importance of learning the Hebrew language, and had many scientific treatises translated into Hebrew.

This openness, however, was not extended to the Chassidic world. The Gra ordered works of the Ba'al Shem Tov burned in Vilna in 1796 and refused to meet with Shneur Zalman of Lyady, the first Chabad Rebbe.

The Gra gave great centrality to the Torah itself, unlike many *chachamim* who focus primarily on Gemarah. Despite his hostility toward *chassidism*, he was well-versed in the literature of the Jewish mystical tradition, the Kabbalah. While he was never elected to any official position, the Gaon was looked upon by all of Lithuanian Jewry, and much of Jewry throughout the world, as their unimpeachable leader. He died in 1797, but his influence lives on.

The Vilna Gaon was the first of a long line of Lithuanian giants. His most gifted student was Rav Chaim of Volozhin. Rav Chaim reinforced the Gra's method of Gemarah study that favored the application of logical reason in place of debate over purported subtleties, *pilpul*.

When Rav Chaim Volozhiner died in 1821, his son, Rav Yitzhak, became head of the Etz Chaim yeshiva. Rav Yitzhak, like his predecessors, was not only a Talmud scholar, but had acquired much knowledge in secular studies as well. He spoke many languages and was well-versed in mathematics. Toward the end of his life, he turned over management of the yeshiva to his two sons-in-law, Eliezer Yitzhak and Naftali Zevi Yehuda Berlin – the "Netziv."

When Rav Eliezer Yitzhak died only a few years later, there was a difference in opinion as to whether the Netziv should succeed him or be passed over in favor of Rav Chaim Volozhiner's grandson – Joseph Ber Soloveitchik. The temporary solution of naming the Netziv as rosh yeshiva and Rav Soloveitchik as his top aide did not work well, and Rav Soloveitchik took the position of chief rabbi of Slutzk.

The families were united by two events: the marriage of Rav Joseph Ber Soloveitchik's son, Rav Chaim Soloveitchik, to the granddaughter of the Netziv, and the appointment of his son-in-law as his deputy and obvious successor.

Rather than a study in dynasties, these events are a remarkable testimony to a succession of true *geonim* who attracted students from all over the Torah world. The intense devotion to Gemarah study and strict attention to personal ethical values set by the

Vilna Gaon, and continued by his successors, constitutes one of the streams of Judaism guaranteeing Jewish continuity.

The grandson of Rav Chaim was Joseph Ber Soloveitchik, the grandfather of Joseph Dov Soloveitchik, "the Rav" of Rabbis Lichtenstein and Riskin.

The above mentioned are only the beginning of a long list of Lithuanian rabbinic giants whose histories make fascinating reading that is beyond the scope of this book. We shall move on after pausing to mention two additional Lithuanian luminaries – Rav Israel Meir Ha-Kohen – the Chafetz Chaim – and Rav Israel Lipkin of Salant, the founder of the *mussar* movement.

With the Russian Revolution and World War I, many Lithuanian Jews saw the writing on the wall. They emigrated in many directions, one of them being South Africa. This refuge, like America, would serve as home for only a few generations, before Jews turned their hearts homeward, many ending up living part of the dream created by Moshko Moskovic.

Lest one think that the success story of Mickey and Yonatan Mirvis is unique among South African Jewry, meet Richard Saevitzon who, in Capetown, was Richard Sloan. The name Saevitzon comes from "*saevitz*" which means "son of Isaiah." A group of twenty people at Johannesburg Yeshiva College planned to make aliyah to Israel together. They all grew up in traditional, but not *frum* families, and were drawn closer to Judaism by the Bnei Akiva organization. Attending Bnei Akiva events was at first nothing more than a social opportunity to be in a Jewish environment.

Within their Bnei Akiva group, especially at summer camps where they went as campers in their younger days, there was a special connection "from afar" with Gush Etzion. They knew the history of the fall of the Gush in 1948, and one of the age groups at the camp was called the "Etzionim."

There were three marriages within the group in South Africa and many had children; this was a time when the idea of aliyah could have slipped onto the back burner. However, true to their dream, twelve of their graduating class from Yeshiva College came on aliyah between 1980 and 1984. Many of them came to an absorption center in Gilo and ultimately settled in Efrat, where they lived within a few minutes walk from one another's homes.

Richard and his wife, the former Cheryl Gantovnik, met through Bnei Akiva. Cheryl was born in Durban. Her father was part of the Jewish emigration from Lithuania to South Africa. There he met Cheryl's mother who is a native of Cape Town. By coincidence, her father and Richard's father had been in the same Talmud Torah class .

Richard has the distinction of being an eldest son of an eldest son of an eldest son. The grandfather was born in Savlan, White Russia, and Richard's grandmother on his father's side was from Mir, which, situated in Belarus, had been part of Lithuania. When World War II broke out, the Mir Yeshiva, headed by Rabbi Eliezer Judah Finkel, moved to Vilna. The escape of the Mir Yeshiva to Shanghai is one of the miracles within the horrors of the Holocaust. Most of the students of the yeshiva went to Brooklyn after the war, where the Mir Yeshiva Central Institute was set up. Rabbi Finkel arrived in Israel to set up the Mir Yeshiva branch in Jerusalem.

Richard, who has a passion for music, established the Efrat Choir during the 1983–1994 time period he and Cheryl lived there. After moving to Ramot in 1994, he established a choir in that Jerusalem neighborhood, a group that has performed all over Israel. Richard and Cheryl have three daughters – Shira, Rina and Tanya – all born in Israel. Richard, an accountant for Kiryat Yitzhak Wolfson, is one of a number of South Africans working in the Wolfson professional building. One South African dentist and several physicians are only a few floors below his office.

Harav Avraham Yitzhak HaCohen Kook, Israel's first Chief Rabbi

Chapter XI
The World View
of the Ravs

RABBIS Amital, Lichtenstein, and Riskin are not authoritarian figures who dictate to their students what to think. Tolerance of all views within a religious Jewish framework is a high value, and we have seen that there can be disagreement on a wide range of issues. However, there is a clear *hashkafa* – view of the world – that runs through the great majority of their students, in particular, and the residents of Alon Shevut and Efrat, in general.

When Rav Amital was taken to a work camp during World War II, he took with him a book of mishnas and a book of the writings of Rabbi Avraham Yitzhak HaCohen Kook, Israel's first chief rabbi. Though Rav Kook passed from this world almost seventy years ago, his passionate Zionism, expressed through a vision that estranged him from many of his fellow rabbis, still burns brightly in Rav Amital and many Israelis who have studied and internalized Rav Kook's message. Who was Rav Kook and what was his message?

Rav Kook was born in 1865 in a remote Russian village. His father imbued him with tales of the chassidim, while his mother came from a long line of *mitnagdim* – those opposed to chassidism. He was recognized before age ten as a prodigy of enormous talents. He studied largely on his own until he was sent to learn at a yeshiva in Lutzin, and then on to the Volozhin Academy under the famous Rav Naftali Zvi Yehuda Berlin.

As a young man, Rav Kook came into contact with *maskilim* – Jews imbued with the spirit of the enlightenment and involved in a broad range of secular studies. Like many of the *Geonim* before him, Rav Kook read widely the works of Nietzsche, Kant, Schopenhauer and other philosophers. However, *limudei kodesh* remained for him the most important learning in his life. He had the privilege of studying with Rav Yisrael Meir – the Chafetz Chaim, who prevailed upon his brilliant student to become a rabbi in the city of Zaumel. There he encountered a great kabbalist, Rav Solomon Eliashiv, with whom he studied the tradition of the Lurianic kabbala, a major influence in Rav Kook's life.

Rav Kook deeply believed in God's revelation through Knesset Yisrael – the entire body of the Jewish people. As opposed to measures of economic and military might, Rav Kook found that the divine spark of the Jewish people nested in its *neshamah*, its spiritual source, its thirst for knowledge of God. Rav Kook wrote explicitly: "The *neshamah* of the individuals derives from the source of the Eternal living in the general treasure, and the totality gives *neshamah* to the individuals. If he wishes to detach himself from the nation, he must detach his *neshamah* from its place in life; therefore the affinity of each individual Jew to the totality is great, and he always commits his life."

Thus, it was no surprise when Rav Kook resisted calls from all over Europe to reside in the most populous areas of Jewish learning. Instead, he came to *Eretz Yisrael* in 1904 to the small city of Jaffa as chief rabbi. He saw in the secular *chalutzim* – pioneers – a manifestation of God's revelation, partners in the building of God's kingdom on earth. He had a five-year period of exile from Eretz

Yisrael when, in 1914, he traveled to Germany to attend a conference. World War I broke out, and he was unsuccessful in his efforts to make his way back to Palestine. Only at the end of the war was he able to return, this time as Chief Rabbi of the *yishuv* – the Jewish community in Palestine.

Rav Kook traveled widely among the secular kibbutzim, many of them highly anti-religious. This brought down on him great criticism from many in the haredi world. His general response is embodied in an assertion, in his well-known *Orot HaKodesh*, that an appropriate fear of sin can too easily pass over into "fear of thought, and once man begins to be afraid to think, he will become immersed in the slush of ignorance that takes away the light of his soul."

While seeing in the secular pioneers a representation of God's redemptive plan, Rav Kook never blurred his central message. He understood the desire of the secularists to become "like other people," yet called their solution to the feeling of alienation among the people of the world a false solution. He did not urge a change in their personal perception, rather he constantly reminded them that this was not the vision of God for the Jewish people. This view of the messianic vision of the Jewish people was shared by many secular leaders, most notably David Ben-Gurion. Israel's mission was unique, not "like all the nations."

It is not difficult to find, in Rav Yehuda Amital, an eloquent extension of the teaching of Rav Kook. The two works he took with him into the evil Nazi camps influenced him to emerge in Israel as a champion of the values that Rav Kook left behind.

In speaking to his students about attitudes toward secular Jews, Rav Amital draws on many sources to teach his students that "a Jew is one who is commanded by Torah. The mere fact of his being commanded makes him a Jew, even if he does not observe." When a convert comes to Judaism, he takes on the peoplehood and the commandments. This, Rav Amital explains, is the root meaning of

Ruth's declaration to Naomi: "Your people shall be my people and your God shall be my God." He points out that the peoplehood affiliation comes first, because only when "your people are my people," can "your God become my God."

As for those who completely reject the Torah, Rav Amital turns to Rav Kook for the judgment that they should be regarded as innocents coerced by the prevailing cultural and general atmosphere. Quoting from one of Rav Kook's letters, Rav Amital cites the following: "But if you think that it is fitting to ignore all those young people who have been swept away from the path of Torah and faith by the raging torrent of our time, then I declare unequivocally that this is not the way that God desires." Rav Amital elaborates by saying: "Let it be borne in mind that the above was said before the Holocaust. What shall we say after the Holocaust? Are we permitted to condemn people who find it difficult to have faith after all that the Holocaust did to Jewish souls?"

Rav Amital differentiates between animosity against Jews for being bearers of Torah, a hatred that once ceased when the Jew gave up his religion, and today's racial hatred:

> Contemporary Jew-hatred is racial, directed against people in whose veins Jewish blood flows, irrespective of whether they live by the Torah or have had themselves baptized. When Jew-hatred is aimed at a person solely because he is a Jew, regardless of his opinions and actions, so should *ahavat Yisrael* – love of ones fellow Jews – also be directed at every Jew solely because he is a Jew, regardless of his opinions and actions. Let no one entertain the notion that someone treated as a Jew by the anti-Semite is going to be treated by us as an outsider.

Turning to life in the modern state of Israel, Rav Amital makes the point that believing that the reestablishment of the State of Israel was the result of the sanctification and glorification of God's name, and that this haven for millions of Jews depends on Israel's capacity to defend itself against its enemies, requires of us to recognize the spark of divinity in every Jew. Rav Amital clearly differentiates the community in which he is a preeminent leader from the religious sectors that do not see modern Israel as part of God's plan:

> If the State of Israel is precious to us, if we have not yet been infected by the "*charedi* heresy" that excluded God from the history of the reestablishment of Jewish statehood and regards it as a purely human act, then we had better realize that the State of Israel is not going to endure if cordial relations do not prevail between all sectors of the nation. Only if Jews relate to each other as brothers, irrespective of ideology, can we maintain this state. Otherwise we live under a threat of destruction.

The Yom Kippur War brought upon the Jewish people a great crisis of faith and confidence. It was a time when spiritual leadership was desperately needed. Rav Amital spoke to his students on November 20, 1973, to help them deal with the anxieties of the war in general, and the specific grief over the loss of their eight fellow yeshiva students who were killed defending Israel.[3]

Rav Amital began by framing the questions: "For the Jew who believes that the events which affect the life of the Jewish people are guided by Divine Providence, it is natural to ask what are the meanings and significance of such events. The question being raised in these times is: What is the significance of the Yom Kippur War?" Rav Amital does not believe that the redemption of the Jewish People requires suffering. "All the misfortunes and sufferings which have afflicted the People of Israel down through the ages – including pre-messianic trials and tribulations which herald a great birth – all these are not inescapable: the birth can come without them."

Given that we are in a time of redemption through suffering, there is an "obligation of moral introspection and reflection on our actions," not those of someone else. Then Rav Amital told his students that "the purpose of suffering is not merely punishment. Suffering both refines and educates, and its educational aims can be far removed indeed from those sins which brought about the misfortune. This process places a man on the path of suffering by inducing in him consciousness and perception in certain areas."

From the same precept that requires introspection and contrition comes the obligation for thanksgiving. "We cry bitterly and we fast," says Maimonides, "and when salvation comes, and rains fall, we sing praises to the Almighty." In a key passage, Rav Amital framed the Yom Kippur War in the latter category:

> We must realize that, despite the sacrifices and the great pain, we have just witnessed a supremely great salvation, and we are obliged to give thanks. If we realized the extent of this deliverance we would sense its messianic base. What happened, happened – we entered this war without a premonition of danger, and therefore, except those who physically experienced the great danger themselves, we cannot feel the extent of the salvation. Even though families mourn, the contrition does not put out of mind the duty of thanksgiving.

Rav Amital said that the Yom Kippur War was an "obligatory war," because it called on Israel to respond "against hostile armies bent on our destruction," and quoting Maimonides: "It is encumbent on every Jew who is able to come to the aid of his brothers in distress and save them from pagan hands." Elaborating on this further, Rav Amital said:

> Any war in Israel is a war in the name of the Unity of God. The nature of the war is unaltered whether those who take part in it recognize its purpose or not. Israel, by its very existence, represents the divine concept of the Unity of God and of his paths of

righteousness and justice. The victory of Israel then is the victory of the divine concept, and any defeat is the defeat of that concept....The war of the gentiles is a war against God; but insofar as they cannot wage war against God himself, they wage war against Israel. War of the Land of Israel is a war on Jerusalem. Only a war against Jewry and against Jerusalem could have united all the Arab States. When we talk of war, we must see things in a biblical perspective, and this recent war takes on a messianic dimension. The phenomenon of war is itself a biblical one – throughout the two thousand years of diaspora we knew no war; much bitter travail, yes, but not war....We cannot view this war as we viewed the calamities of the days of dispersion. We must recognize the greatness of the hour in its biblical perspective, and this can be seen only in the light of the Messiah.

The Yom Kippur War "removed the war from a local and transitory plane to a messianic, an historical and revolutionary dimension." Rav Amital pointed out that all of the world was involved in the war. Not only the Arab States were involved, but the superpowers, and all oil-consuming nations. Some involvements were positive, some negative, whether it was the direct aid from the United States to Israel and of the former Soviet Union to the Arab states, or whether it was the nations of Europe refusing to let planes flying emergency help to Israel cross their airspace. The danger and loss of life obscured the higher meaning:

Few people as yet recognize the extent of the salvation. There have not been many wars in Jewish history like this one: a war of the few against the many. This time each tank was opposed by a hundred – such a ratio never occurred before. If we consider that the enemy was stopped in those sectors of the north and the south in which our forces were inadequately deployed, it was clearly a command from above. If we listen to the accounts of senior officers, we will understand that the proportions of the salvation in this war have a great miraculous aspect, and it is this that gives the war its messianic dimension.

The Gemarah, Rav Amital said, teaches that war is the beginning of redemption. Maimonides voiced the connection this way: "If there appears a king of the House of David, steeped in the Torah and observant of the Law, the oral as well as the written, like David his forefather, and he compels Israel to follow and keep the Law, and he wages war in the name of the Lord – it will be considered that he is the Messiah."

In a message ringing true for all Jews now, early in the twenty-first century, just as for those who faced the aftermath of the Yom Kippur War, Rav Amital summoned his students to a higher level:

> We need great faith, great confidence and strong nerves in these times. Perseverance and strength are what are demanded from our leaders. We must be encouraged in our faith and our confidence. We are enjoined to live in the belief that, since the beginning of the Return to Zion, there is no turning back. Things are sometimes veiled from us, but there is no regression. All the paths – paved and unpaved – lead towards the redemption of Israel. The footsteps of the Messiah approach with suffering, and sometimes by a circuitous path. We should know from the outset that, with the approach of the Messiah, from every woe will come salvation, and salvation comes out of suffering. The Land of Israel is paid for by suffering, but thereby it is paid for in full.

After the end of the Yom Kippur War of 1973, Israel was in possession of even more territory than it conquered in the Six Day War of 1967. Such a situation had never been encountered in the history of the Jewish people, so one could only draw on religious sources for guidance. Rav Amital is repelled by those who cite halachic sources as rejecting any territorial compromise. His view is clear and has been for many years: The three basic values in Judaism, in order of their importance, are (1) the Jewish people, (2) the Torah, and (3) the land of Israel.

Given the order of these priorities, the decisive factor in any proposed negotiations is the good of the Jewish people. The concept of peace is of great concern for the Jewish people, but within this concept are imbedded important concepts, such as the spiritual and moral image of the people and the need for unity of the Jewish people, those in Israel and those in the diaspora, those who are *shomrei mitzvot* – followers of the commandments – and those who are not. To Rav Amital, putting control of all of historical *Eretz Yisrael* first stands the order of priorities on its head.

The unity of the Jewish people demands an understanding not only of any given religious point of view, but an understanding of all Jews. Rav Amital makes a distinction between secondary issues, such as closing places of entertainment and public transport on Shabbat, and larger issues. The secondary issues annoy non-religious Jews, but will not cause a deep split among the Jewish people. However, if halachic reasons are cited to justify the imposition of what would be seen as extreme solutions to existential issues crucial to the future of the State of Israel, then a great potential danger would confront us."

The expression of such views takes a great deal of courage. Rav Amital has been exposed to harsh criticism from within the religious community. Many who agree with him remain silent. Yet Rav Amital's position has been vindicated by the fact that on many occasions decisions have been made by the government that reflect his position, and those with more rigid views have continued to serve as part of government coalitions that enforce those positions.

The assassination of Prime Minister Yitzhak Rabin was an enormous trauma for Israel, especially for the religious community. Yigal Amir, a former *hesder* yeshiva student (not at Yeshivat

Har Etzion), was the accused assassin.[4] Rav Amital responded
swiftly to help his students deal with the trauma, and the accusa-
tions, in a constructive manner. The day after the assassination, the
students were assembled at Yeshivat Har Etzion. Rav Amital told
them: "Today, we are stunned and shattered, depressed, disgraced
and shamed, pained and sorrowed, by the abominable murder of
the Prime Minister of Israel, in this *"reishit tzemichat ge'ulatemu"* –
the dawn of our redemption." Quoting Maimonides, Rav Amital
said:

> In his commentary on *Sefer Devarim,* specifically, the section
> commanding us to choose a king, the Rambam states that whom-
> ever the Jewish people choose is the choice of God. If God had not
> approved, the election would not have succeeded. This horrible
> act, directed against the kingdom of Israel, is also an assault on
> the kingdom of God. It is an assault on the entire people of Israel,
> not only because of the act itself, but because one man cannot say:
> "I will decide for everyone; I have the right to assault the anointed
> of God, chosen by the people, a man who dedicated his entire
> life to the Jewish people." How many merits he had! Even if one
> disagreed with all his policies, the role the Prime Minister played
> in the Six Day War alone is sufficient to atone for anything else
> he might have done…"

Rav Amital told the assembled students: "We are obligated to
rend our garments over the desecration of God's name. Have we
become like Sedom, do we resemble Amora? The Jewish people,
who taught the world absolute morality, beginning with the pro-
hibition on murder; the Jewish state, the only democracy in the
Middle East, a nation founded on the vision of redemption – now
resembles some Third World banana republic. This obligates us to
keri'a, if not to rend our clothes, then to rend our hearts. What has
happened to us?" In closing, Rav Amital implored his students:

In the battle for the Jewish soul of the nation, we have received a stab in the back. Now we have to prove that *"deracheha darchei noam"* – "[the Torah's] ways are ways of pleasantness." We must constantly remember that every action, every appearance can – and in our situation, must – be a *kiddush Ha-Shem*. We will increase unity and avoid hatred; we will find the ways to see the positive aspects of every Jew; we will pray to God that he will protect us and purify our hearts from hatred, envy, and slander; and we will continue to build this great undertaking that is the work of the hands of God – the return to Zion – until we witness the coming of the redeemer, speedily in our days, Amen.

RAV AHARON LICHTENSTEIN

Rav Lichtenstein followed Rav Amital in speaking to the students at Yeshivat Har Etzion following Rabin's assassination. He first stressed "the personal aspect: the family's loss, even when there is a national, public aspect." In terms of the national shame, Rav Lichtenstein had just visited the brother of "the Rav," Rav Aaron Soloveitchik. He pointed out that Soloveitchik's "fierce opposition to the peace process is well-known," yet "as soon as I walked in, he repeated over and over – 'a badge of shame, a badge of shame.' For two days he hadn't slept out of shame and humiliation. This shame – that our state, our people, should have fallen to such a level, should be felt by everyone: religious, secular, right and left."

Rav Lichtenstein described the special worry for those, such as everyone at Yeshivat Har Etzion, who lived in settlements:

> There is a special source of worry for those to whom the settlement of Yehuda and Shomron is important. This is paradoxical, since the fiercest opposition to his leadership arose precisely from those ranks. It is clear, though, that within his government, Yitzhak Rabin was the one who, more than anyone else, cared for and protected settlements, and hence will be missed by us, more

than by others, for just this reason. But even more, within the
issue of the peace process, there is importance not just to what is
given back, but also to how it is given back – not just the contents
of policy, but to how it is carried out. In this respect, objectively
speaking, if we rise above the opposition to the policy, Rabin was
the proponent of this policy as a necessary compromise.

Rav Lichtenstein addressed Rabin's statements which belittled
"the value of Eretz Yisrael," but said: "I am sure he regretted [them]
afterwards. Nonetheless, his genuine feeling for our values will be
missed by all of us, whether we support territorial compromise or
not."

When Rav Amital was asked to join the government Shimon
Peres put together after the Rabin assassination, he did so out of
a sense of mission, but stated explicitly: "I was not excited about
becoming a minister." Even though Rav Amital's time at the yeshiva was to be greatly reduced by his new role, Rav Lichtenstein
wholeheartedly supported his decision. He told the students that
while "there are those who will claim that the immediate loss to
the religious community, the Yeshiva and to Rav Amital personally, far outweigh the possible benefits of his newly acquired position…the chances of some success, particularly on issues relating
to the Jewish people and Jewishness, are high. A feeling of responsibility is what motivates Rav Amital. Rav Lichtenstein movingly
described the characteristics that made Rav Amital the perfect
choice:

> He is one of those rare individuals who is able to synthesize vi-
> sion with reality, idealism with pragmatism, and dreams with
> the ability to bring them to fruition. His background will enable
> him, b'ezrat Hashem, to connect with the various segments of the
> nation, especially at a time when the growing divisiveness has
> become so critical…his standing in the religious Zionist commu-

nity, as well as his reputation among the non-religious populace, command respect and admiration, and thus he is able to serve as a uniting figure of the different sectors of the Israeli public.[5]

Rav Aharon Lichtenstein is one of the most erudite thinkers in the Jewish world. He is reserved, but not quiet. He is scholarly, but not aloof. He may appear to be a loner, but he is passionately involved with the people he touches on a daily basis. He is deeply committed to Jewish values, while alert to the influences that threaten to dilute them. He teaches heads of yeshivas and the youngest students in Yeshivat Har Etzion. The depth and breadth of his thought touches on the issues that inspire the religious world, as well as those that trouble the religious world. His basic reference is to the Torah and all that derives from it.

In a series of lectures to first year Yeshivat Har Etzion students from the diaspora, Rav Lichtenstein addressed some of the fundamental issues confronting them. He delineated three areas shaping our world:

"the universal demands placed upon one simply as a human being; the demands of a Jew; and (3) the responsibilities of a ben-Torah, one who makes Torah study a central part of his life and embodies its values."[6]

Rav Lichtenstein cites God's charge to Adam from the book of *Bereishit* – Genesis:

'The Lord God took the man and placed him in the Garden of Eden to cultivate it and to guard it.' These two tasks, to cultivate it and to guard it, have different connotations. One, *le-shomrah*, is largely conservative, aimed at preserving nature. It means to guard the world, to watch it – and watching is essentially a static occupation, seeing to it that things do not change, that they remain as they are. This is what Adam was expected to do, and part of our task in the world is indeed to guard that which we have been given: our natural environment, our social setting, our religious heritage.

"At the same time," Rav Lichtenstein points out, "there is the task of *le-ovdah* – to cultivate it which is essentially creative: to develop, to work, to innovate." These mandates apply both to the society in which one lives and to the "human personality itself," and this quickly introduces a basic conflict:

> Now, this is of great importance and needs to be stressed, because we are dealing here with a fundamentally religious perception that runs counter to the notions prevalent within the widely secular society in which we find ourselves. The essence of modern secular culture is the notion of human sovereignty; individual man is master over himself, and collective man is master over his collective. This creates problems as to where the line is to be drawn between individual and collective man, and that issue is the crux of much of modern socio-political theory – when the state can and cannot interfere. But the common denominator of all these discussions is that they think fundamentally in terms of human sovereignty, the question being whether you speak of humanity or of a particular person. From a religious point of view, of course, *eilu va-eilu divrei avoda zara* – both approaches are idolatrous. Here one establishes individual man an idol, and then one idolizes, in humanistic terms, humanity as a whole. The basis of any religious perception of human existence is the sense that man is not a master: neither a master over the world around him, nor a master over himself.

This view does not negate the notion of private property. Rav Lichtenstein points out that "the notion of property is a very central concept in *halachah*, and large sections of the Talmud are devoted to it. Rather, what this means is that the notion of property is never absolute. It is always relative; ultimately, '*La-Hashem ha-aretz u-melo'ah* – the Earth is the Lord's and all that it holds.'" The quote is from *Psalms*, 24:1. Man's command is not only to watch over what he has been given, but to work it, improve it. Rav Lichtenstein cites a story in a midrash of a conversation between the Roman governor Turnus Rufus and Rabbi Akiva:

> Turnus Rufus asked Rabbi Akiva, 'If God wanted man to be circumcised, then why did He not created him that way?' Rabbi Akiva responded, 'Bring me some wheat.' Then he said, 'Bring me a loaf of bread.' He asked, 'Which do you prefer to eat, the bread or the wheat?' 'Naturally, the bread,' Turnus Rufus replied. Rabbi Akiva retorted, 'Do you not see now that the works of flesh and blood are more pleasant than those of God?' There is a certain audacity here, but these are the words of Rabbi Akiva! What you have here is an assertion of human ability and grandeur, and of human responsibility to engage in this kind of improvement.

Counting himself among "humanists," Rav Lichtenstein says that humanists "talk a great deal about man placing his imprint on the world…I am not talking only about secular humanists; I mean religious humanists within our world as well. The religious world puts a clear emphasis on work, not just as an act of *tikun olam* – perfecting the world – but as a value in and of itself. A midrash tells of Abraham, when he was still "Abram," doing God's bidding to leave his native land and go "to the land which I will show you." When he arrived at a place where people were idle, he kept walking, but when he saw people busy at work, he knew that this was "the land which I will show you."

There is a delicate balance to be maintained. While not arguing for an ascetic way of life, Rav Lichtenstein warns his students that the religious world is not immune from the seductive music of hedonism. "In the last decade or two, a whole culture has developed geared towards *frum* Jews, where the message is enjoy, enjoy, enjoy, and everything has a *hechsher* – kosher certificate – and a super-*hechsher.*" The idea that man is born for pleasure is one to be avoided for anyone aspiring to be a follower of Torah.

Rav Lichtenstein directly tackles the issue of whether God's covenant with man contradicts the universally regarded values of mankind. Are universal values overridden, or are they in harmony with the covenant? He answers:

> …we do not believe that what existed until now was merely scaffolding which was needed until the building was complete, but now that the building is finished, everything else is insignificant. Instead, we assume that whatever commitments, demands and obligations devolve upon a person simply as a member of the universal community, will apply to him within his unique context as well…Whatever is demanded of us as part of Knesset Yisrael does not negate what is demanded of us simply as human beings on a universal level, but rather comes in addition.

The belief that the Torah's demands do not negate universal human values, and that one can indeed speak of religious humanism, separates the centrist religious perspective from the *charedi* perspective. However, the gap between religious humanism and secular humanism is significantly larger than that between centrist Orthodoxy and the world of the *charedim*. Rav Lichtenstein returns over and over again to the theme that "we live in a world wherein the ideal of self-fulfillment is taken for granted. Sometimes this assumes a more obviously negative guise, such as when people espouse an ideal of pleasure-seeking. However, it can also assume a noble, moral tone: every person has a right and a duty to develop his inherent capabilities…But surely, Judaism perceives human existence differently: Our perception is that a man or a woman is fundamentally a being who is commanded, who is called, upon whom demands are made. And the fulfillment of these demands may or may not be congruent with self-fulfillment."

Is there anything that is unique to Judaism that separates it, not only from the non-religious world, but also from other religions? There is no simplistic answer to such a complex question, but Rav Lichtenstein asserts that this aspect of being *metzuveh* – called, commanded – "is what religious existence in general is about, and certainly applies to Judaism more than to most other religions."

Most Jews, raised Jewish outside the Orthodox world, understand a mitzvah as a "good deed." Yet, here we have a radically different understanding of the word. The root of the word is *tzav* and, in modern Hebrew, a *tzav giyuss* is an induction order into the army. The biblical understanding of the word is the same, and here we can begin to understand the world of the religious Jew, even a "centrist" orthodox Jew. Rav Lichtenstein makes the case starkly:

> Now, to live the existence of a *metzuveh*, of one who is called and commanded, involves to some extent the subjugation of ones inclinations and desires. A *metzuveh* leads a theocentric rather than an anthropocentric life. He is guided by God's will, not by his own likes and preferences. 'Nullify your will before [God's] will' (*Avot* 2:4) constitutes a cardinal tenet of Judaism....If you are commanded, you do not pick and choose among commands – that would be living an anthropocentric life, placing yourself in the center and building everything around yourself...Another important ramification is in the area of learning. The Gemarah in *Eruvin* (64a) compares a person who says, 'I like this *sugya* (subject) and I don't like that one: I'll learn this section of the Gemarah, but I won't learn that one', to a person who consorts with prostitutes. Similarly the Gemarah in *Sanhedrin* (99b) has very sharp words for a person who learns Torah occasionally and does not set fixed times for study: He is 'a heartless adulterer.' How can learning Torah be compared to committing adultery

or consorting with prostitutes? The essence of fornication is self-fulfillment. A man wants to extract sexual pleasure from a woman, and after he has used her to satisfy himself, he has no responsibility towards her and continues on his way. Tomorrow he'll find another woman…A person has to subject himself to Torah and not to subject Torah to himself.

Rav Lichtenstein quotes approvingly the Robert Frost poem, "*Two Tramps in Mud Time:*"

My object in living is to unite
My avocation and my vocation
As my two eyes make one in sight.

He continues:

I agree that a person should strive for this goal – he should enjoy his work as if it were a hobby. In a parallel sense, a person indeed should enjoy his *avodat Hashem* – serving God – and feel fulfilled by it – but not because these were initially his own desires and intuitions. These started as being God's will, which you are commanded to fulfill. But you have molded yourself in such a way that you find joy in responding to command; your self-fulfillment comes from living the life of one who is called, rather than the life of one who is guided solely by his own inner feelings.

A large percentage of the students at Yeshivat Har Etzion will become educators and, in that context, will naturally continue studying and teaching Torah. However, many will go into other professions. Are they then finished with the study of sacred texts? The answer, for most, is no. Rav Lichtenstein talks to his students about this issue. In a Mishnah in Tractate *Avot* of the Gemarah, it is written, Shammai says: Make your Torah *keva*." *Keva* is a Hebrew word which connotes "fixed, permanent."

Rashi gives two interpretations, one being that one should not set aside times for Torah, but study it continuously the entire day, while the second is that one should set times to learn four or five chapters every day. Rav Lichtenstein explains that the first interpretation does not relate literally to sitting and learning all day, but to an attitude that conveys the sense: "Do not set aside time for Torah like you set aside time for tennis. Rather, make it an important factor around which your day revolves. How much you will actually be able to learn depends upon circumstances – where you are, what other responsibilities you have, etc. But in terms of your attitude, your commitment to Torah is rock-solid; it is the framework through which you view your life." How does one translate this centrality of Torah into action?

> Though a person may thirst for Torah, this longing still needs to be translated into practical terms. If you remain with nothing more than this general thirst, it is entirely conceivable that nothing will come of it – it will remain hazy and fuzzy, but will not translate into actual limmud Torah. This is where the second element in Rashi comes to the fore: 'Set aside time to learn four or five chapters a day.' While you should set no upper limit to your learning, surely you cannot make do without setting a lower limit, a daily minimum. In order to give firmness to your commitment to Torah, you must set minimal designated times for learning.

The focus is not on quantity of time, but where Torah study is in one's value system, one's priorities. Rav Lichtenstein translates this into practical terms:

> It may be that the axiological centrality of Torah will not necessarily translate into its being quantitatively that to which you

devote most of your time. When one plans his personal budget, or when a government plans a national budget, there is little disposable income left after one has factored in the various expenses of the necessities of life. Similarly, after one factors in the time he must devote to fulfilling his responsibilites and obligations, how much 'free time' is left? But the test is precisely what a person does with whatever time is left to him. He doesn't have a choice about going to work; he has to make a living. But when he comes home, he can decide whether to read the paper and watch television or to sit down and learn.

Another part of the *keva* is that one is obligated to absorb the learning, make it a part of him. Rav Lichtenstein points out that, in the discussion throughout the Gemarah of the different aspects of *keva*, the Gemarah is not just talking about the scholar, or the yeshiva student, but to all Jews. Rav Lichtenstein elaborates that this is a "radical demand" on the layman, but it is clear that it is the intent of the Gemarah to make this demand. "I know many are troubled by the question of how to develop the requisite passion and yearning for Torah. People would like to find some formula which would enable one to attain this automatically." While not having a formula, Rav Lichtenstein does have advice for his students:

> Perhaps it is most important to stress that this is not a phenomenon we can regard in isolation. The extent to which a person is committed to Torah is very much a function of his commitment to God, and therefore it is related to the place of *avodat Hashem* – serving God – and *yirat Shamayim* – fear of Heaven – within his life in general. There may be some people who simply have a fancy, as it were, for Torah. But for most people, if the deph of *yirat Shamayim* is lacking, then it is unlikely that, of all the things to which they are exposed, "an ox which gores" is going to interest him the most....Inasmuch as a person is involved with Torah

because he sees it as divine, as *Torat Hashem*, then the extent to
which he relates to God is also going to have a great impact on
how he relates to Torah.

Rav Lichtenstein advises that one should also relate to the
problem of developing the extent of a place in his life for Torah
by studying the writings of our great scholars of the past. "Not all
of these are equally effective for everyone, but surely in some way
one should try to encounter them. Some people may find that the
Vilna Gaon speaks to them, others may read Rav Kook, and others
the Ramban, Nachmanides."

For his yeshiva students, Rav Lichtenstein adds a deeper level
to the impetus of *keva* in Torah study. The Gemarah "speaks of 'a
person who hears something from a sage in the *beit ha-midrash*.'
This distinguishes between an '*adam* – person' – and a '*chacham* –
sage.' Of course, a *ben-yeshiva* should strive ultimately to be not
just the *adam* who listens to the *chacham*, but to be the *chacham*
himself."

RAV SHLOMO RISKIN

Rav Shlomo Riskin's world-view is one of inspiration, faith and deep
belief. Much of this he imbibed from his maternal grandmother
who came to the United States from the shtetl of Lubien, Poland in
1922. Her children and grandchildren were assimilating. Rav Riskin
was the only one to attend a yeshiva, and this was a departure from
how he had been raised.

At Lincoln Square Synagogue in New York, Rav Riskin had one
of the most visible, celebrated and vibrant Orthodox congregations
in the United States of America, yet he moved to a craggy, lonely
hill in the Judean wilderness. Why?

On a conscious level, the biblical commandment "And you shall
inherit the land and dwell therein" (*Numbers* 33:53) was the first

motivating factor. But it was not only because of the formal command, which at least according to Nachmanides, applies to every Jew in every generation. It was also due to my perception that the newly established State of Israel exultantly confirms the eternity of the Jewish people and demonstrates that our ancient prayer for the ingathering of exiles and the rebuilding of Jerusalem had not been uttered in vain. Moreover, I yearned to join in the most magnificent adventure of our people in two thousand years. I could not escape the sense that, after May 14, 1948, whatever happens in the diaspora to the Jewish people is at best a footnote to Jewish history, whereas in Israel we are meriting the chapter headings.

Just after he came to Efrat, Rav Riskin had an experience which confirmed why he was there. "The streets were not paved, there was only one public telephone which usually didn't work, and during a difficult winter we suffered the cold virtually without heat or electricity." One night, a man knocked on his door and told him he had guard duty. They began to talk about what they did before they moved to Israel, and this was the man's story:

I grew up as a Christian, and even went to church every Sunday with my father, mother and brother. For some strange, inexplicable reason, I always felt a close tie to Israel. In fact, for my high school senior paper, I wrote on the burgeoning Jewish state. Upon graduation, I felt I needed a break from formal study. When the Yom Kippur War broke out, and Israel called for volunteers to work in the kibbutzim to take the place of the men on the front lines, two Christian friends and I were accepted for a kibbutz in the Galil. I quickly learned the language, fell in love with the land and the people, began to read Jewish history and theology, and, since I wanted to keep kosher, became a vegetarian. I had even begun to try to observe the Sabbath, when some members of the kibbutz suggested I enroll in the ulpan for converts in kibbutz Kfar Etzion, only a few minutes from Efrat. I did so and was soon given a date for mikveh immersion and conversion. I realized I had better at least discuss it first with my parents.

The young man's parents sent him a ticket to return home. He told them he wanted to convert to Judaism and live in Israel. His mother broke into a sweat and fainted:

When she was revived, she looked into my eyes. 'You need not convert,' she said. 'You need not convert because you are already Jewish. You are Jewish because I am Jewish. When the Nazi policeman murdered my parents in front of my eyes, and threw me into a cattle car for Theresienstadt, I felt in my gut that, if one holocaust occurred, another was more than likely. I only knew that I did not want my children and grandchildren to suffer as I had suffered. I therefore took an oath in that cattle car – if I ever emerge from this hellhole alive, it will be as a Christian and not as a Jew. Well, I got out alive; I don't know how or why. I had no one to answer to, for all my blood relatives were destroyed. Until this moment, the only one who knows of my Jewish background is your father. If you wish to rejoin the religion of my parents and grandparents, may the God in whom I cannot believe bless you and keep you.

"When I heard this story," Rav Riskin says, "I understood why I had come and why I would never leave. The words which flashed before my mind's eye and seared themselves into my soul when this man ended his tale were those first prophesied by Moses in God's name more than four thousand years ago: 'Even if you be scattered to the ends of the heaven, from there will God your Lord take you and bring you up…to the land of your fathers.'" These promises require faith, yet faith is rewarded when one sees the promises fulfilled in one's own time. Rav Riskin tells the following story about the power of faith:

> Two chassidim always visited their Rebbe on the festival of Suk-kot, and each year, on the way, they stopped at the same inn. One year the innkeeper approached them humbly. 'You know that I am not a *chassid* or a disciple of your Rebbe,' he said. 'But I have a great favor to ask of you. My wife and I have been married for ten years, but unfortunately we have not been blessed with a child. Please ask the Rebbe to pray for us.' The chassidim agreed to do so, and the next morning the innkeeper's wife began parad-ing around the neighborhood with an expensive baby carriage. When her friends gathered around her to wish her mazal tov, she explained that she was not yet with child but would soon be, because the Rebbe was going to pray for her. The two chassidim were embarrassed, because they knew that prayers do not always bring the hoped-for result, but they said nothing and continued on their journey, faithfully performing their mission when they arrived at the Rebbe's court.
>
> The following year, when the chassidim returned to the inn, the baby's circumcision was in progress. The innkeeper of course was quite grateful and treated them as guests of honor. Later on, one of the chassidim went to see the Rebbe. 'You didn't even know the innkeeper,' he complained, 'but I am your trusted disciple. Yet I have been married for twenty years and I don't have a child. Every year for the past twenty years, I've made the same request of you, and my wife still has not conceived. Rebbe, is it fair?' The Rebbe took his disciple's hands and looked deeply into his eyes. 'During all those twenty years, did you ever buy a baby carriage? How great was your faith compared to that of the innkeeper's wife?'

As Rav Riskin explains: "For the past two thousand years of life in the Diaspora, the Jews have always had the baby carriage ready.

Despite oppression and discrimination, they never lost faith; they always believed that there would be ultimate redemption."

Just as Rav Amital deeply believes that one's Torah study cannot be genuine if he "does not hear the cry of a baby" – is not aware of and alert to the problems of the world outside the *beit midrash* – so too does Rav Riskin believe this. He tells the story of two great *Geonim* to illustrate the point:

> The Vilna Gaon, a man who studied Torah twenty hours a day, committed to every nuance of Jewish law, as master of kabbalah, a giant among giants, approached the equally illustrious Dubno Maggid. 'I feel so close to God; is there anything you can tell me which will help me obey the commandment I find most difficult to keep – how to repent?' Replied the Dubno Maggid: 'You think I'm so impressed that you sit in the house of study all day, surrounded only by holy scrolls? Go out to the marketplace, meet your fellow Jews in the midst of all their concerns, fears and worries. Take the risk of involving yourself in their difficulties and then let's see what kind of saint you'll be.' The Vilna Gaon began to weep. He understood that true commitment means risking a little bit of your own eternity so that other Jews will come a little bit closer to God.

In relating a midrash about Abraham, Rav Riskin makes a crucial point. After Abraham fed his guests and treated them with great warmth, and they thanked him, Abraham would say: "Don't thank me, thank God." But what happened when one traveler said he does not believe in God and that he had Sarah to thank for the food? Rav Riskin proceeds: "No sooner does the guest exit than a Heavenly voice booms: 'You have some *chutzpah*. I have allowed this man to walk My earth and have fed him for forty years, and you get hysterical after one meal? If you want a clue as to what you did to him, how abused and manipulated this man felt when you

threw him out, look into the future, old man, and see how, because
of you, your children will become slaves and learn what it means
to be despised." And the lesson to modern Jews?:

> If there is anything observant Jews have to learn, God is saying,
> it is how to expose and not to impose. And if you want a formula
> for this, a methodology, all you have to do is look at the interpre-
> tation of Maimonides: 'Reprove your friend but do not 'bear his
> guilt.' In other words, when you talk to him, don't do it in a way
> which will boomerang back at you with the additional burden
> of a new sin, that is, just as it is a command to bring him closer
> when he wants to listen, when he's asking questions, and if you
> don't try to answer them, it's your sin and not his, it is equally
> important to be silent if your words would only embarrass him
> or turn him further away.

Rav Riskin tells a story about the legendary Chafetz Chaim,
Rabbi Israel Meir Kagan, which illustrates how a pious Jew can
reach a "fallen" Jew without castigating him. The story is about
a student of the Chafetz Chaim who had been caught smoking
on Shabbat. This mandated expulsion of the student, but first the
Chafetz Chaim asked his staff to send the young man to his house.
In a very short time, he convinced the student to change his ways.
Rav Riskin told this story to an audience in Miami and commented
that he would give anything to know what the Chafetz Chaim said
to turn the student around. As he was telling the story, he noticed
a man in the front row begin trembling uncontrollably. After the
lecture, the man ran up to Rav Riskin and said: "I'm that man. It
happened to me!" They took a walk on the beach, and Rav Riskin
heard the following:

> It was in the late 1920s. I was very young, and the Chafetz Chaim
> was already in his eighties. He was also much shorter than I,

hardly coming up to my shoulder. I never really spoke to him. He stayed in his grocery store for the first hour of the day, and then he would go home and study, but when he was in the street, he would never let anyone say hello to him first; he always greeted the individual first. So I got greetings from him, but I never spoke to him. When I was told he wanted to see me, I didn't know what to expect. When I walked into his house after being summoned, although I was dazed by the prospect of being addressed by the Chafetz Chaim himself, I couldn't help noticing how poor everything seemed. In the room where I was standing, there wasn't one piece of furniture that was not broken. But before I could get my bearings, there was the Chafetz Chaim right in front of me. I am sure he must have looked at me, but all I remember is a face larger than life. Suddenly he grabbed hold of my hand, clutching it tightly, and out of his mouth I heard the word 'Shabbos' said with such feeling, as if he were uttering the name of the most beloved object in the world. Then there was silence, and then he began to cry – not sniffles, but streams of tears, and the tears from his eyes fell on the palm of my hand. Even if I live until one hundred and twenty, I will never forget the feeling of how hot those tears were. They actually burned my hand. And then I heard one more word, 'Shabbos,' with the same awesome sense of love and anguish and, still holding my hand, he took me to the door.

Rav Riskin's message to the Miami audience was: "It is very easy to throw stones, but it is very hard to be a Chafetz Chaim. Religious Jews must never stop feeling the pain of watching fellow Jews violate the Sabbath, but if we shout, then we must shout with tears coming out of our eyes like the Chafetz Chaim, and not like some fanatical, bloodthirsty excuse for a Jew. When stones become tears, and threats are refined to a trembling voice that can teach everything about who we are as Jews with only two syllables, then I am not worried about the rift between religious and non-religious Jews."

Though Rav Riskin was educated by Rav Soloveitchik and always looked up to him as his mentor, Rav Riskin also draws frequently on Israel's first Chief Rabbi, Rav Avraham Yitzhak HaCohen Kook, for inspiration. Rav Kook was denounced by many rabbis of his time for his tolerance to those who desecrated Shabbat. In a letter written to the Chief Rabbi of Safed, Rav Kook reminded his detractor that there were two covenants in Jewish history. The first was the covenant between God and Abraham, and the second was the covenant with the Jewish people as a whole at Mount Sinai, and not all of the people at Sinai were holy and pious men and women.

Rav Kook cited a passage from the Gemarah (*Sanhedrin 99*) that foresees the *mashiach* riding on a donkey. The donkey, not having split hooves, is a non-kosher animal. Yet there is a mitzvah to redeem a first-born donkey, just as there is a mitzvah to redeem a first-born son. The donkey, Rav Kook wrote, has an inner sanctity, and *mashiach* will come because of Jews with inner sanctity, not those who observe the Sabbath but have no inner sanctity. Rav Riskin found a passage in a posthumously published article by Rav Kook that elaborates on this point:

> The souls of those sinners of Israel in the generation of the footsteps of the Messiah – those sinners whose souls are linked with love to those issues affecting all of Israel, the land of Israel and the renaissance of the nation of Israel, the souls of those sinners of Israel are more perfect than the souls of the religionists who do not have that feeling for the good of the majority and the building of the nation in the land.

Rav Riskin is a perfect example of the fact that one person can bring a family back from the brink of assimilation. His parents were secular and the grandchildren from both his maternal and paternal sides were rapidly assimilating into the open, free society of America. He returns, over and over, to memories of his maternal grandmother, a deeply religious woman, who was the person who influenced him in the direction he chose.

> She was a remarkable woman, steeped in Jewish knowledge and commitment, who came to Brooklyn, New York, from the shtetl of Lubien, Poland, in 1922 and died in 1960 without ever having learned to speak a proper English sentence. Her world remained the world of Yiddish and Hebrew, the world of the prayer book, the Bible, and her closest friends were all from the same shtetl in which she grew up. Her synagogue was called Etz Chaim Anshei Lubein – Tree of Life of the People of Lubien…the congregants sat in the very rows in which they had sat in the synagogue in Lubien, and their burial plots (the Lubien section of the Washington Cemetery in Bensonhurst, Brooklyn) were parceled out accordingly, one's ultimate resting place alongside those with whom one had spent "divine time" on the Sabbaths and festivals.

Through his grandmother, Rav Riskin learned that her father, Rav Shlomo HaKohen Kowalsky, had been the *dayan* – Jewish judge – of Lubien and had lived a very long life – one hundred and fifteen years according to family tradition. His first three children being girls, he had no boys to teach Torah, so Rav Riskin's grandmother, thirsty for learning, studied with him. He ultimately had many sons, but continued studying with his daughter. Thus, she had much to pass on to her grandson, Shlomo, who is named after her father:

> Grandma had a marvelous way of making the Biblical personalities live. She skipped nothing, and I learned the "facts of life" from the various Biblical passages and prohibitions I studied with her….She especially loved to describe the courtships of our patriarchs and matriarchs and specifically the love affair between

Jacob and Rachel. 'That's how it was with your grandfather and me,' she said…And so we would spend each Friday night with delicious food, delightful stories, interesting Torah, and I felt transported to an almost magical *shtetl*, Lubien; I felt I really knew the streets, the smells, the people – even better than the Bedford Stuyvesant area wherein I lived.

In 1993, Rav Riskin had an opportunity to visit Lubien when he was invited to join the March of the Living pilgrimage to Europe. He found the small town of three hundred and fifty families and sought someone who might have known the Kowalsky family. One resident of the town led him to another, until he finally located a ninety-one year old woman 'who always lived among the Jews.' "Pan Kowalsky, Pan Kowalsky," she greeted him, then shared her memories:

> Your great-grandfather was the *dayan* of the town. Of course he was a very old man when I was a young girl; everyone said that the angel of death forgot about him. My brother was the mayor of Lubien, and so the rabbi, Rabbi Petrovsky, and, for the more important issues, your great-grandfather, would visit in our home….Your great-grandfather was a very wise man, a great judge; but he insisted on working for his living, and until he died he sold hay and oats to the neighboring farmers.

The kind Polish woman related what happened to the community when World War II broke out:

> The synagogue was a beautiful building. In 1939, when the Nazis came in, every single Jew – men, women, and children – went in to pray. The Nazis set the building on fire, and refused to allow our Fire Department to put the fire out. Not only the synagogue, but the entire block went up in smoke. Your great-grandfather's house survived the fire, as it was on the other side….The Jews were all

taken away and killed. The last Kowalskys were tailors. Maybe a few survived, but most were killed. The Jewish cemetery used to be on the other side of the lake, opposite the Christian cemetery. The Nazi's razed it to the ground. They took the gravestones and used them to pave the paths of their concentration camps.

Rav Riskin went to the site where the Jewish cemetery had been and said "*El Male Rachamim*" for his great-grandfather. The trip accomplished its purpose. In fact, Rav Riskin says: "I had traveled to Poland to find Lubien, to recapture my childhood, to discover my roots. But where is Lubien? I understand now that Lubien is not near Wroclaw; it's not even near Wloclawek. In fact, Lubien is not in Poland anymore. Lubien is with me and my Israeli grand-children, here in Efrat."

From his grandmother, Rav Riskin also, as a twelve year-old boy, learned something of the universality of Jewish ethics. His grandmother had a boarder at her house that everyone referred to as "the goy." He was often at the table for festive meals. As Bed-ford-Stuyvesant gradually made the transition from a "once-proud enclave of upwardly mobile Jewish immigrants" to a non-Jewish crime-ridden area, the family approached Rav Riskin's grandmother about moving. "She was a realist," he relates, and told him: "I know that it is necessary for us to move, but what about the goy?" It was only after she had found a suitable place for him that she agreed to the move.

Chapter XII
The Importance of Moshko

T HE IMPORTANCE of the individual in history is widely debated among historians. Those who minimize the role of the individual in history stress the inevitability of historical processes. While it is acknowledged that the individual in history has choices, it is also asserted that these choices are strictly limited by the social, economic and political forces that propel history forward.

On the other hand, many historians ascribe great importance to the role of the individual in history. Lucy Dawidowicz, a noted Jewish historian, wrote: "By attributing historical responsibility to the medieval mind, the Renaissance spirit, the Industrial Revolution, mass culture, secularism, or inevitability, some historians have managed to evade the attribution of human responsibility for the occurrence of historical events....History is at bottom an account of what men did and achieved, and the historian's task is to untangle that meshwork of human character, behavior, and motive whose intertwining creates the very material of history."[7]

Many other historians share this view. John Clive is "suspicious" of historians "who think that they can formulate historical laws,

thereby eliminating the unique, the contingent, the unforeseen."[8]
Barbara Tuchman agrees, recording her mistrust of "history in
galon jugs, whose purveyors are more concerned with establishing
the meaning and purpose of history than with what happened."[9]

In totalitarian societies, history is distorted by outright fabri-
cations. In democratic societies, historical distortion is primarily
a function of what the historian leaves out. Carr tells us that it is
the historian "who decides to which facts to give the floor, and
in what order or context."[10] Dawidowicz makes the crucial point
that when historians knowingly or unknowingly omit from their
historical writing an account of any given course of events, those
events disappear from history.

One has vivid images of the personalities who were prominent in Israel's triumphant 1967 Six Day War – the image of Moshe
Dayan surveying the battlefield and the kudos heaped on Yitzhak
Rabin, military chief of staff, who coordinated the battles on three
fronts. From an historical viewpoint, Israel's victory was an imperative for survival; one could reasonably contend that it would have
been achieved regardless of individual leaders.

There was much to preoccupy Israeli leaders in the aftermath of
the Six Day War. Moshe Dayan, shortly after cesssation of hostilities,
declared that Israel would ultimately have to give up the territories
conquered in the war. Establishing a yeshiva in Gush Etzion did
not appear on the government's list of priorities. Building the city
of Efrat, a city that did not exist before the war, certainly was not
among the plans, even the dreams, of the country's leaders. For
the general Israeli population there was no historical imperative
for these projects; it is not difficult to imagine the development of
modern-day Israel without Alon Shevut and Efrat. It *was* a historical imperative for Moshe Moskovic.

Though Moshko had his work cut out for him to get government cooperation, and five long years were to go by before all the
approvals were in place for Efrat, there is today a population center

for Torah study in the Gush that is a model for the country and the world. Hopefully, the interviews reproduced in this book provide the reader with person-to-person familiarity of the *kippa s'ruga* community. They are people with an eye and a heart open to the world. One can see that, while they value and love their culture, they are ready to deal with Jews from non-Orthodox communities. More than that, they have a highly-developed sense of *clal Yisrael*, and *clal Yisrael* means all Jews.

An extension of the evaluation of the individual's place in history is the study of "the hero" in history. The historian Sidney Hooks points out that, while there are limitations to the use of the term "heroes," it is natural for man to seek positive role models:

> Many of the might-have-beens of history were beyond human control. It is hard to see what human beings could have done to realize these might-have-beens...other might-have-beens were within human grasp....[some] were lost becaue of the failure to be more intelligent, more courageous, more resolute – sometimes a little more of each. The triumphs of intelligence will never violate natural and social necessities. Intelligence and will supply, by their own effort, some of the conditions upon which the transition from the "might be" to the "is" hangs....Among the most poignant tragedies of history are those in which men have cried "impossible" too soon and, for want of vision, have summoned up energies sufficient to win the day – too late.

Hooks sums up by addressing the moral responsibility and the qualities of "the hero" in history:

> Moral responsibility in history consists in being aware of the relevant ifs and might-be's in the present, and choosing between alternatives in the light of predictable consequences. We may lose even after we have chosen intelligently and fought bravely...but

intelligence and sustained courage will win much more often than drift and fitful bursts of effort. If there is any ethical imperative valid for all historical periods, it is awareness and action.[11]

Generalizations are often over-used and mis-used in history, but Hooks left us a study for the ages. He did not know Moshko, but his model describes Moshko perfectly. Alon Shevut and Efrat were candidates for "might-have-beens" in history, but they became realities because Moshe Moskovic was "more intelligent, more courageous, more resolute" than all of those who stood in his way. Moshko is one of few men who can say of their aspirations: The reality is greater than the dream.

Endnotes

1 Knohl, Dov, compiler and editor, *Siege in the Hills of Hebron* (Thomas Yoseloff, New York), 1958, p. 31.

2 The book was published in Hebrew, but an English translation is in progress.

3 From the archives of Yeshivat Har Etzion.

4 The official version of Amir's guilt was widely accepted until some years later, when it was called into question.

5 From the archives of Yeshivat Har Etzion.

6 These lectures have recently been published in a book: *"By His Light: Character and Values in the Service of God* (Alon Shevut: Etzion Foundation, 2002).

7 Dawidowicz, Lucy, *The Holocaust and the Historians* (Cambridge: Harvard U Press, 1981), p. 146.

8 Clive, John, *Not By Fact Alone* (Boston: Houghton, Mifflin, Co., 1989), p. 115.

9 Tuchman, Barbara, *Practicing History: Selected Essays* (New York: Ballentine Books, 1981), p. 35.

10 Carr, E.H., *What is History?* (New York: Vintage Books, 1961), p. 89.

11 Hook, Sidney, *The Hero in History: A Study in Limitations and Possibility* (New York: The John Day Company, 1943), p. 146.

Glossary of Terms

Ba'al tshuvah – an incompletely observant Jew who adopts a totally Torah observant lifestyle

Beit midrash – the central study hall of a yeshiva

Charedim – religious Jews, often identified by their blacks hats and coats, who are more insular than the religious Jews of the *kippa s'ruga* community

Chevruta – a number of students studying together; in the *beit midrash*, most often just two students

frum (yiddish) – an adjective describing one who is oberservant of the commandments

Gemarah – part of the Talmud, it is the exposition of the Mishnah. The compilation of the Gemarah took place in the period 250–500 C.E. This term is often used to denote Talmud in its entirety – Mishnah and Gemarah

Gush – a Hebrew word meaning "bloc." The term "The Gush" is most often applied to Gush Etzion

Halachah – Jewish law derived from the Gemarah

Hashem – a Hebrew term literally meaning "the name," this is the term often used in speech and writing by the religious community to refer to God.

Kippa S'ruga – a crocheted skull cap, a term often used as a symbol for the type of religious Zionists who are the topic of this book

Kollel – a group of men, of marriageable age, studying together after completion of yeshiva. Among them are married and single men, some preparing for *smicha*, some studying Gemarah for its own sake

Limudei Kodesh – studies of Jewish sacred literature, in contrast to the term "*limudei chol*" which refers to secular studies

Midrash – a type of rabbinic literature, often thought of as imaginary stories about biblical figures. However, the literature is far more than that, including extensive "talumudic-type" exegesis of the Torah

Mishnah – the first of two parts of the Talmud, it is a concise statement of Jewish law. The mishnaic period lasted roughly from the beginning of the common era to 250 C.E.

Rosh Yeshiva – head of a yeshiva; the plural form is *rashei yeshiva*

Shas – an acronym for *Shishah Sedarim* (six orders); it refers to the six orders of the Talmud

Shi'ur – a Hebrew word meaning "lesson," often shortened to "shir"

Smicha – rabbinic ordination

Talmud – Jewish body of law comprised of the Mishnah and Gemarah

Tanach – the complete work of pre-Talmudic Jewish works; the term is an acronym for "Torah (Five Books of Moses)", "Nevi'im" (prophets), and "Ketuvim" (hagiographa – psalms, proverbs, Job, Song of Songs, Ruth, Lamentations, Ecclesiastes, Esther, Daniel, Ezra, Nehemiah and Chronicles)

Torah – "the Torah" is the Five Books of Moses, the Jewish bible; when one speaks of learning "Torah," the reference can be to any and all of the sacred Jewish works

Index